Wil Anderson is the host and executive producer of the ABC's popular and long-running *Gruen* and new hit *Question Everything*. He is a Helpmann Award–winning stand-up comedian who has also received the People's Choice Award at the Melbourne International Comedy Festival (MICF) a record six times, selling more tickets than any other act in the history of the festival. In 2022 his show *WILOGICAL* won the Director's Choice Award at MICF and Best of The Fest at the Sydney Comedy Festival. Wil currently hosts the popular podcasts *TOFOP, FOFOP, 2 Guys 1 Cup AFL Podcast* and *Wilosophy.*

I AM NOT FINE, THANKS

THANKS

WIL ANDERSON

ALLEN&UNWIN
SYDNEY·MELBOURNE·AUCKLAND·LONDON

First published in 2022

Allen & Unwin
Cammeraygal Country
83 Alexander Street
Crows Nest NSW 2065
Australia
Phone: (61 2) 8425 0100
Email: info@allenandunwin.com
Web: www.allenandunwin.com

*Allen & Unwin acknowledges the Traditional Owners of the Country
on which we live and work. We pay our respects to all Aboriginal and
Torres Strait Islander Elders, past and present.*

 A catalogue record for this
book is available from the
National Library of Australia

ISBN 978 1 76087 894 8

Set in 12.5/19 pt Minion Pro by Midland Typesetters, Australia
Printed and bound in Australia by Griffin Press

10 9 8 7 6 5 4 3 2 1

 The paper in this book is FSC® certified.
FSC® promotes environmentally responsible,
socially beneficial and economically viable
management of the world's forests.

For Irene and Winnie

CONTENTS

1

CANCELLED

I had just walked off stage at the Adelaide Fringe when I found out that the Melbourne International Comedy Festival was not going ahead. I had been expecting the bad news, but when it arrived it still didn't feel real. These days every city has its own comedy festival of some kind, but Melbourne is 'The Festival', and now, along with the Australian Formula One Grand Prix, it was one of the first major events to be shut down. The irony was that there had been nonstop stories in the press about comedians and what lines they could and couldn't cross. Every interview I was doing would inevitably contain the question: 'Are you worried about being cancelled?' Little did we know that all live comedy was about to be cancelled.

It was a shock, and there was natural fear and anger from my clown community, but we all understood why it needed to be done. Comedy likes to pretend it can be dangerous, but suddenly and unexpectedly it most definitely was. In the shadow of a global pandemic, gathering people in a poorly ventilated room to force them to expel fluids from their mouths as often as possible didn't really seem like a responsible night out. In fact, the funnier you were, the more likely you were to be a super-spreader. Comedians like to say that they 'killed', but I'm pretty confident most of them don't actually want anyone to die. If nothing else, it is a bad business model to kill off your customers. I work for the ABC, so I have already lost a percentage of my audience to natural causes. I can't afford to lose any more.

I was disappointed but I didn't have any sense at the time that everything had changed forever. Maybe this is too much to ask, but I feel like life-changing moments should feel like life-changing moments. They should come with some sort of trumpeter and an announcement: 'From this moment on, your life will never be the same again.' Turns out sometimes life-changing moments don't come with a bang, they come with a resigned shrug. Things changed so quickly, and in some ways so permanently, that it is hard to remember what normal really felt like back then. All I know is that there were some things I did without thinking that I will never do again.

Five days before Melbourne was cancelled I was doing a Sunday afternoon line-up show with other comedians at a suburban pub in Adelaide. It was a fun gig, but being a pub, the room we were performing in hadn't been purpose-built for comedy. I am not complaining—most places you perform in as a comedian aren't purpose-built for comedy. For the rest of my shows in Adelaide I was performing in a tent in the middle of an amusement park, so I was grateful that today I had walls and a roof and didn't have to time my punchlines between teenagers screaming on a roller-coaster.

The room was a long thin space that held a couple of hundred people with an aisle down the middle for them to access their seats. As a comedian it's not ideal to have an aisle down the middle of a show, as it means the main place you would normally perform to has no audience sitting in it. It also makes it very hard to stage dive at the end of a successful set. Most importantly, if something happens in that aisle it is likely to catch your eye.

The other problem with the setup of the room was that there were only two ways in, one door right at the back and one right at the front, which meant that once the show started a patron entering from the front would have to walk past the stage right into the performer's eye-line to get to their seat. For this reason, once the show kicked off most people would only enter from the door at the back. Most.

I was the final act for the afternoon. About five minutes into my 20-minute set, one bloke carrying six beers burst through the front door and started slowly walking across the area in front of the stage. He immediately had my attention, because he had everyone's attention. Every single eye in the room was on him, but he didn't notice because he was staring at something much more precious to him: the beers. I'd never seen such laser focus. He did not want to spill even one single drop. If you want to be happy in life, find someone who stares at you the way this man stared at his tray of beer.

I tried to get the audience's attention back on my jokes, but to no avail. I was fighting a losing battle. I had lost them to something more fascinating. 'Sorry, Wil, I know you are trying to entertain us with your carefully crafted jokes and satirical observations about society, but this guy is trying to balance at least two more beers than he should have comfortably attempted on a tray. We need to see how this ends.'

I didn't blame the crowd. I got it, I was fascinated too, and that's what I love about stand-up comedy, when something happens in the room that will never happen again. So I figured if you can't beat them, join them. I took the microphone out of the stand and stepped off the front of the stage into the aisle and started following him. I don't know what I was thinking; I wasn't really, I was just in the moment. I didn't know the destination, but I had set out on the journey. I expected it to be a short trip: surely you would only come in the front door in this situation if your seat was right down the front? Surely.

He walked past the first row, the second row, the third row, and kept walking. So I kept walking too. We were now already far enough back that he should have definitely entered through the rear door, and he didn't show any signs of slowing down. When he got to the middle of the room I couldn't believe this was still happening. I thought about heading back to the stage. But just as I was about to retreat, the spotlight caught the top of his bald shiny head and it seemed like a sign. I felt like a wise man following a star, although I am sure that some would mount the argument that this story does not involve a wise man, or a star.

He kept walking, and walking, and walking. There was tension and amusement in the room; everyone was on the same page except this one man who was still focusing 100 percent on the tray in front of him. I was now starting to worry that he was just going to walk straight down the aisle and out the back door, which would have been one of the ballsiest moves of all time.

Luckily he finally started to slow down and find his row, which was three from the back of the room. Three. It was clear to everyone there was no way he should have ever come in the front door, but his magical mystery tour was not done yet. You see, he was not sitting on the aisle of his row three from the back of the room. No, his seat was deep towards the wall. He started climbing over people, still balancing his beers like he was completing the final leg of *Australian Ninja Warrior*. I couldn't stop now, not when we were so close to the end, so I followed him into the row, also climbing over people. It was only then, when he had sat down in his seat and distributed his beers, that he noticed me.

At this stage I was practically on top of him, trying to still do stand-up comedy while I was basically giving him a lap dance. Less Magic Mike, more Tragic With Mic. As I gyrated in his lap I joked, 'I guess we're not too worried about Covid here. Is this social distancing?'

Then I did something. Something I probably should not have done then, but definitely would never ever do again. One of the things I love about live comedy is how you can take a group of people who might have nothing in common if they met in the foyer and unite them in a community with a laugh. Even better if that moment is unique to the gig and there is a buzz in the crowd that they know they are seeing something they will never see again. And at least from me, I can guarantee they will never see something like this again, because here is what I did.

Feeding off the energy and laughs in the room, I said, 'We're not afraid of some germs, are we? We are not afraid of Covid, are we?' And to emphasise the point, I raised my hand, pretended to lick it, and then . . . patted him on the head. What was I thinking? I am an award-winning stand-up comedian and here I was on a Sunday afternoon in an Adelaide pub patting a bald guy on the head. Who am I, Benny Wil? Even worse, the audience loved it.

I think about that moment a lot. How quickly the world changed. At the time everyone in the room—including, I should stress, Beer Man—thought what happened was funny. We had all experienced a moment together. Something just for us. Five days later, if I told someone I had climbed into a stranger's lap, licked my palm and patted them on the head, they would have had me arrested for committing a hate crime. Lucky comedy got cancelled or I might have been. 'Did you hear about Wil's gig? He killed. Literally, gave a guy Covid straight through the top of his skull. Apparently that is where you are most susceptible.'

I knew that nothing was going back to normal, and if normal was patting a stranger on the head for laughs then maybe normal wasn't all it was cracked up to be anyway. Sometimes life-changing moments don't come with a bang, they come with a slapping sound.

2

TIMING

At the end of 2019 I finished a regular commercial radio job and planned to spend all of 2020 doing stand-up. I was so excited about throwing myself back into the world of live performance, I was taking not one, not two, but three different shows across Australia and hopefully around the world. I didn't know much, but I was certain that 2020 was going to be the best year of my life. What could possibly go wrong? They say the secret to comedy is timing. They also say that comedy is tragedy plus time. They say a lot of things and I haven't had enough time to find that funny yet.

On the upside, I remember saying that I wanted to recapture the way it felt when I first started, and my wish came true. More true than I could have ever imagined. Little did I know how much it was really going to resemble what it felt like when I first started—a long time between each gig and extended periods of unemployment. There was even a moment when I considered dusting off my old material about being on the dole, except that there weren't any gigs anywhere for me to do it.

The very first joke I ever told on stage, more than a quarter of a century ago, was all about my experience of being unemployed. It went something like: 'I hate how society labels unemployed people as dole bludgers. That's because we don't know them personally. They are anonymous. We can label them. If you know them, you know their individual struggle. You empathise with how they found themselves in this situation and how desperately they want to get out. That's why I believe we should take a lead from World Vision and introduce a Sponsor A Dole Bludger program. Every month they get their money, and you as a taxpayer get a little picture of them in line down at the CES. In return for your support, they write you a letter and let you know what has been happening on *Ricki Lake*.' (For the younger readers, the CES was what they used to call Centrelink, and *Ricki Lake* was what we used to watch before Netflix.)

April 2020 would have been my 25th year in a row performing at the Melbourne International Comedy Festival. Melbourne is the first city where I ever saw stand-up comedy live. It's the city where I sat in a room with my mum at seventeen years old watching Billy Connolly entertain 3000 people of all ages with nothing more than his imagination and liberal use of the word *fuck* and thought, 'This is what I want to do with my life.'

All I ever dreamed of when I first started doing comedy was that one day I would get to do a show at the Melbourne International Comedy Festival. In fact, I loved the festival so much that when I was an unemployed stand-up I used to go into the festival office with biscuits my sister had baked to bribe them for free tickets to shows.

Fast forward a quarter of a century and more people have seen me do my job at that festival than anywhere else in the world. It's the first thing that goes in my diary every year, and everything else I have done for almost half my life has been centred around it. It's not an exaggeration to say it was my anchor. Then, unexpectedly, my anchor was gone, and I was adrift. What would my life look like if I wasn't doing a show at the festival? I guess I was finally going to find out.

I never set out to do the festival 25 years in a row. When I started, once would have been enough. Once *was* enough for a few of my friends and relatives who came to see me the first year and have never come back since, no matter how many free tickets I have offered them, they were so scarred from the experience. I get that, I would have been terrible, but do they really think I have not improved since then? I do want to say, if they are reading this, I've got better! I promise. The festival wouldn't have let me keep coming back if I had stayed that crap. I am much funnier now, I'm doing hilarious things like patting a man on the head.

I had never set out to write a new show every year. It just happened without me really thinking about it. I figured that if they had gone to the effort of putting the festival on, it would be rude of me not to put together a show. And then, after a while, it was just what I did. And what I planned to keep doing until I ran out of Wil puns for titles. I'd always talked about having a year off, but when it came to the crunch I didn't want to miss out.

A friend did ask me about ten years ago if I would ever take a year off and I said, 'Maybe if I make it to 25 in a row. That seems like a good number. In fact, 25 in a row and I might not just take a year off, I might quit comedy altogether.'

So 2020 would have made it 25 in a row. Then Covid happened. Coincidence? I don't believe in God, but if there is one it's good to know he is a fan.

Yes, only a stand-up comedian could make a pandemic all about themselves.

3

FARM

The start of a global pandemic was an interesting time to move to the anti-vaccine capital of Australia. When Covid first hit, I lost a month of work in a minute and a year of work in a week, so I decided to get out of the city and move to the farm. *A* farm, that is. Not *The* Farm. Things weren't that bad that they had to send me to The Farm, where I could run free with all the other unemployed comedians. No, Wil, your career is not dead. It's just at The Farm. It's happy there.

The farm in question was not really a farm in any real definition of the word. It was a house in the country with a bigger garden than usual. There were some pumpkins growing in the yard, but that was only because they sprouted out of the bottom of the overflowing compost bin, so I think claiming the title Pumpkin Farmer would be a stretch.

In fact, to call it a farm is a massive insult to my parents, who are real dairy farmers. At the very least it's milk-culture appropriation. But where I went was definitely the country. The nearest town was 20 minutes' drive away and had a population of around 4000, a magical community I love called Mullumbimby.

You may have heard of Mullumbimby. It is of course renowned as the scientific heart of Australia. Yes, they love science in Mullum. They love it so much they have their very own artisanal brand of science, called pseudoscience. The great thing about pseudoscience is that while dumb old science only has answers to some questions, pseudoscience has a solution for every problem. All you have to do is swallow a packet of pseudoephedrine for it to make sense, and that won't be the hardest thing you are asked to swallow.

As someone who has always believed that the boring old-fashioned scientific method was the best one we had to organise our curiosity, it was definitely a shock to the system to realise, in a time when we needed science more than ever, that I was becoming part of a community where that wisdom was not the prevailing one. As a middle-aged white cisgender Australian man, I had never been a minority before and I have got to say I did not like it. Not one bit. People don't listen to you, they constantly discount your opinion, and are always correcting things you say with 'Well, actually . . .' It's no good. Ten out of ten would not recommend. I don't know how the rest of you have put up with it for so long without saying anything.

Of course, there was an upside to living in that part of the world during a pandemic, and that was short lines for the vaccines. Very efficient. People would ask me which vaccine I got and I would say, 'All of them. I just go through the bins out the back of the medical centre at the end of the day: jab, jab, jab.'

To be fair to the locals, they did not need the vaccine in that particular community, because they had something much more powerful than any vaccine cooked up in a lab by a bunch of eggheads. (Side note: they also did not trust eggheads, because as committed vegans they would only take advice from tofu-heads.)

They didn't need vaccines because they had Apple Cider Vinegar. I don't know if you have heard of the wonders of Apple Cider Vinegar, but if you spend any time in the Northern Rivers region of New South Wales, you will. In fact, you will find that 95 percent of the conversations you have will somehow involve this miracle product.

You have a sore throat? What you need is some hot water and Apple Cider Vinegar. You have high blood sugar? Have a shot of Apple Cider Vinegar after a meal. You smell bad? Dab some Apple Cider Vinegar in your armpits. I see you are having a salad—you know what will make a lovely vinaigrette? Bird shit on the windscreen of your car—you know what will get that straight off? Apple Cider Vinegar. I noticed you're also out of fuel, so what I recommend you do is fill up the tank with Apple Cider Vinegar. You get 1000 kilometres to each bottle.

They love it so much that one day when someone was extolling the various uses of the product I attempted one of my trademark comedy jokes and said, 'Actually, my problem is that I spilled some Apple Cider Vinegar on my rug and now I can't get the stain out,' and without missing a beat they said, 'Oh, you know what will get that out? More Apple Cider Vinegar.'

It was brought up so regularly I started to think: is this town sponsored by Apple Cider Vinegar? What I do know is if they wanted people to get vaccines in those parts they should have been more creative and changed the name of AstraZeneca to AppleCiderVinegar. People would have been lining up around the block to take it. 'Did you hear the great news? They're injecting it now.'

4

ROAD

I took the AppleCiderVinegar vaccine, by which I mean I received its big-city cousin, the AstraZeneca. I didn't worry about any risks real or imagined; we were in crisis and if I could help others by taking a small risk then I was happy to do it. If I ended up growing a third arm or something, I would use it to high-five the other people who had also done their bit when I passed them in the street.

I was in an age group that qualified for the Pfizer shot and I had booked in my appointment at the soonest availability. Then the prime minister called a press conference, and I paid attention. I paid attention because this was a time of national crisis and the prime minister of the country was . . . in the country. There was not a Hawaiian shirt or ukulele to be seen. I knew Scott Morrison must be serious.

I can't remember the exact wording of what he said but it

was something along the lines of, 'You know earlier when I said it wasn't a race for the vaccines, well it seems like everyone else has been racing and so we are way behind, so we need to start racing, even though I reiterate that it is definitely not a race. Anyway, it would be handy, even if you're booked in for the Pfizer, to see if you could take the AstraZeneca because we have got heaps of that for some reason but definitely not because we kept telling people it was no good and ruined its reputation, and stuffed up the whole rollout, so big favour, talk to your doctor and see what the risks of AstraZeneca are for you.' That may not have been exactly what he said, but that was what I heard.

Showing how powerful the words of a leader can be in a time of national crisis, I did as our prime minister requested, called the medical centre in Mullumbimby and booked in to talk to my doctor. They had an appointment for me: two hours later. To be fair, there is less waiting time for real medicine in that town than there is for alternative medicine. If the prime minister had suggested that I talk to my homeopath about the risks, it would have been a three-month wait.

Two hours later I found myself in my doctor's office and one thing was immediately apparent. He had not been as moved by the prime minister's words as I had, because he had been at work all day, not watching television at home like me, and I had only visited him a week earlier when I booked in my original shot. He looked at me, slightly confused, and asked, 'So why are you here?' And I said something that was the truth, but as soon as the words exited my mouth I knew how ridiculous they sounded: 'Because the prime minister told me to come.'

He told me to sit down and I explained the situation. I wasn't worried about taking the vaccine; I knew there was a small risk but I was willing to take that risk for the greater good. The prime minister had said to ask my doctor what the risks of the AstraZeneca were for me, so here I was, just a boy standing in front of his doctor asking him what the risks of the vaccine were.

My doctor paused as he took all that in and then calmly asked, 'Did you drive the winding road into town today?'

He knew that I probably had. It was the only way directly from my house, and 'direct' is doing some heavy lifting in that sentence. The road winds through the hills. It is scenic, surrounded by trees with occasional views to the coast, but it's sometimes a little scary with a few stretches where you could easily go over the side. It's one of those roads that's more corners than straights, which feels like a fitting preparation for spending time in Mullum. I nodded.

He said, 'Well, there is about 500 times more chance you will die in a car accident on that drive home than there is you will have any major side-effects from the vaccine.'

That made me feel great about the jab, but pretty shit about the apparent death drive I had to make it home. I had already driven that road more than 500 times, so I was living on borrowed time. (By the way, I know that's not how that statistic actually works, but my mind was racing.) I was now convinced I was going to die on the road home and, even worse, my arm would be sore from the needle. That's probably why I would veer off the road. Now, I knew I couldn't say any of this out loud to my medical practitioner, so instead the question that escaped my mouth was, 'If I die in a car accident on the way home because my arm is sore from the vaccine, do you think they will call that a road accident or a vaccine-related death?'

He looked at me and asked, 'Are you okay?'

The lie started to form in my mind and my mouth, and I was about to reply that I was 'fine, thanks' but instead I just shook my head.

He said, 'I think you need a laugh. The great comedian Adam Hills is in town tonight. You should go and see the great comedian Adam Hills, he never fails to cheer people up.'

I said, 'But Doctor, I am Adam Hills.'

He could tell I needed some more reassurance about the jab. 'If it makes you feel any better, I took the AstraZeneca and I am ten years younger than you.'

It did make me feel better about the vaccine, but it didn't make me feel better that I am now old enough to have a doctor who is a decade younger than me. That can't be true. I am still young and cool, right? I am on Triple J. It is impossible that I have a doctor who is ten years younger than me, because I am only 29. My doctor must be Doogie Howser, which ironically is a reference you probably won't understand if you're under 29.

I ended up getting the vaccine that day, and made it home safely with only minor side-effects the next day. The major side-effect was that I have never driven that winding road again in peace without that statistic bouncing around my head.

5

BOOSTED

I booked in as promptly as I possibly could for my booster shot, first name on the list as soon as I qualified. I got up early and braved the death drive so I could get the first appointment of the day. The clinic doctor administering the shots was one I hadn't met before but was a charming eccentric who sat me down, slapped my arm like I had once slapped a bald man's head in an Adelaide bar and announced, 'There you go, I'm done!'

Done what? Done preparing me for the jab and now was going to give it? He hadn't jabbed me, had he? I had looked away because I don't like needles. But I didn't see a needle. Had I missed it? I must have, I guess. He must be really efficient at his job and the slap was a way of covering any pain. I guess that makes sense, right? I didn't really know what to say. I didn't want to accuse him of faking it. So instead I asked, 'Should I stick around for fifteen minutes?'

This is what they had asked us to do the previous times. He said, 'You can if you want, but no-one is checking.'

I stayed anyway, because to be honest I was confused. Not as a side-effect of the vaccine but confused as to whether I had actually received the booster in the first place. I still wasn't entirely sure. I removed the bandaid on my arm and tried to see if I could spot a prick hole. I took a photo of my arm on my phone and enlarged the focus. When that didn't clear it up, I kept pressing the area, hoping to get some pain that indicated the booster was in there.

My brain started to race, even as I tried to reassure it that it was not a race. Was there a chance that I hadn't got the needle? Had I accidentally stumbled into a fake doctor's office where they were faking giving people vaccines? No wonder he had said I didn't have to stick around; there is not much risk of side-effects if you haven't been given the vaccine. While I waited my fifteen minutes I decided to check if my vaccine certificate had been updated, so I logged onto the app and it had been. But even that did not reassure me. It made me think: what if this is part of the scam? I left and spent the rest of the day checking if my arm was sore, and then, when it finally was, worrying about whether it was only sore because I had been poking it too much.

Luckily I woke up the next morning feeling terrible. I felt awful, mostly for doubting the doctor, because from the side-effects I was experiencing it was clear I had definitely received my booster. I might be the first person who was ever happy to get side-effects from the vaccine. 'Oh, I have flu-like symptoms, nausea and a massive headache . . . What a relief.'

I was happy to take the vaccines, but not everyone I knew was happy that I had taken them. One of the things I learned from my new community is that you can think a person is a good person even if they have what you think are bad ideas.

One of the people I like most in the town is an older lady who is an incredible contributor to the community but also happens to be one of the biggest anti-vaxxers. I like talking to her in general, but every time I got my vaccine it would become a talking point and we would have a mostly good-natured back and forth about it. Mostly good-natured because I would keep the majority of what I was thinking to myself and just listen. Sometimes I think we forget that when someone has a world view we don't agree with, we don't always need to argue with them. Sometimes we can just listen. You don't need to agree, but you can try, in the words of one of the great philosophers, George Michael, to listen without prejudice. You've just got to have faith, and most importantly remember to wake me up before you go go.

However, when I got my booster shot, the tone of our conversations changed. I don't know why but this time she was genuinely angry at me. She said, 'So you lined up and got your booster, did you, sheep? Is your stomach full from swallowing the narrative? You're just a compliant sheep.'

I could see there was a theme developing but she was not done. She had another question: 'What are you going to do, sheep? Are you just going to line up and keep taking your shots every six months because there is Covid in the community?'

All I could think to say in response was, 'Yes . . . *Baaaaaaaaaa!*'

Am I going to line up every six months for my free government medicine in the middle of a global pandemic? Yes, yes, I am. And if that makes me a sheep then call me Wool Anderson. I'm Baa Baa Wearing All Black Sheep. I think it's a scientific miracle that these vaccines even exist, and on top of that we can get them for no cost. The least I can do is take them, after all the effort that went into them, so they can have the best chance to work. And I will have yours too if you don't want it. Boost me up. I will be a Booster Juicer.

I didn't say any of this, of course; I just nodded.

She said, 'Surely if the vaccines worked, you wouldn't have to keep taking them!'

Surely? I am not so sure. Not sure that's how all vaccines work. In fact, now that I think about it, that's not even how a lot of life-saving medicines work. Or, to be perfectly honest, how most things that keep you alive work. I had some water this morning, but I am going to have to drink some more later or I will die. That doesn't mean that water is no good and it doesn't work. Water is good. I am about 60 percent water, and at the moment you are 60 percent bullshit. Now, you might need to sit down for a minute because I am about to run you through breathing, and it is really going to blow your mind. This is *Through the Looking Glass* stuff. No wonder there are so many advertisements for breathing classes on the local community noticeboard. It makes a lot of sense now.

Of course, I did not say any of this. I bit my tongue and nodded again.

Luckily, my contribution wasn't really necessary. She had a point to make and she was just warming up. She looked at me accusingly and said, 'You just like the needles, don't you? You are basically a junkie!'

And I couldn't help myself, I started laughing. Not in a mean-spirited way; how could I be mad at that argument? That is not just a fundamental misunderstanding of vaccines, but also a fundamental misunderstanding of drug addicts.

Now, I should point out I have never tried heroin. One reason is that I actually don't like needles. The other reason is that I have never really seen any good Yelp reviews of heroin. Part of the problem with heroin, from my understanding, is that once you have some heroin you want some more heroin and then some more heroin. However, if I heard that every six months the government was going to get a doctor to give you medically tested heroin, and then you would be full of heroin and wouldn't want any more for about half a year . . . then I would probably try heroin. If I did that three times in eighteen months, I wouldn't call myself a junkie. That is disrespectful to actual heroin addicts who earned the right to call themselves that. I would say I was dabbling in the horse.

But that's not even the biggest misunderstanding. The biggest misunderstanding is that needles are the big appeal of heroin, rather than say, I don't know, the heroin. If it was just the needle that was appealing, then *Trainspotting* would be a much lovelier movie about four friends who get together every eight weeks to donate blood. They just can't get enough of those needles and they love saving lives. They did Choose Life, theirs and the lives of countless others they help with their donations, and now that they are not doing all that heroin, they actually have some time to go and spot some trains after.

Fade to black. Iggy Pop's 'Lust For Life' plays unironically.

6

FINE

Someone asked me the most confronting question recently. I was in a local shop buying some groceries and then out of nowhere the person who was helping me just dropped this bomb and nearly knocked me off my feet.

'How are you?'

How am I? How am I? How do you think I am? I know in the Before Times the tradition was to reply, 'I'm fine, thanks.' Then you would ask how they were, and they would reply, 'I'm fine, thanks.' And then we would all get on with our lives. But I can't play my part in that pantomime anymore. I cannot say, 'I am fine, thanks,' because (spoilers) I am not fine, thanks.

And to be perfectly honest, if I asked someone how they were at the moment and they replied, 'I'm fine, thanks,' I would think that person was a psychopath and start slowly backing out of the room, keeping eye contact at all times. I would report them to the authorities: 'I am not sure what the crime is, but I asked them how they were and they said they were fine so I think you need to keep an eye on them.'

How could you be fine? Did you throw your television away in January 2020? Did you just wake up from a coma this afternoon and not have a chance to catch the news yet? Because if that is the case I am about to give you a quick *Previously on McLeod's Daughters* of what has been going on for the last couple of years. There has been a global pandemic that has changed everything forever, most of it not in good ways, and it is still not over despite people pretending it is. Climate change is a Code Red for humanity. World War 3 might have started, it's not even making the news most days, and the person in charge of the good guys is a comedian. How am I? I am not fine.

I think we need to take a break from asking people how they are unless we have the time to hear how they are. Maybe we could have a period when we just answer with the truth? 'How am I? Thanks for asking. I am fucked. Everything is fucked. How could you be anything but fucked? And now I feel even worse because it sounds like I just said butt-fucked. I am so sorry. Anyway, how are you?' And they would probably say, 'I am fine, thanks.' And we would get on with our lives.

I think that before this happened I would have generally described myself as a glass-half-full type of person, but everything we've been through has changed that. Well, not entirely. I am still glass-half-full, but I now assume the glass will be half full of poison, and then when I have finished my poison colada someone will smash my empty glass into my face.

I've never really been one for inspirational mottos. My main problem with self-help isn't that I don't believe that those lessons worked for the author, but that the author is not me. In the words of our Lord and Saviour Jesus Christ, '*The world don't move to the beat of just one drum / What might be right for you may not be right for some.*'

But I also never had a problem with self-help until the pandemic. Now, every time someone offers the slightest bit of inspirational advice I almost snap. There was a moment recently when a lovely glass-overflowing type finished our interaction by grabbing my hand and whispering, 'Remember, you are awesome and you are doing great!'

That is a nice thing to say to another person, but all I could think was, you don't know me, I am not doing great, the other night I cried during *The Mighty Ducks*. (I'll be honest, even when times are good I cry during *The Mighty Ducks*.) Even if I was doing great you don't know what I am doing great at. For all you know, I could be a serial killer who is awesome at killing people in a serial fashion and then doing great at disposing of the bodies and not getting caught. You know what, I was thinking about giving up murdering, but your words of encouragement have come at a great time. Thank you, now where is my shovel?

I've never been a huge fan of inspirational slogans—my car's rear windscreen and my couch cushions are all a blank slate—but I'd always appreciated other people's positivity, until the pandemic. Suddenly every bumper sticker seemed like a personal challenge. I spotted one that said, 'Never forget that you are a warrior', and all I could think was that that car didn't know me at all. I am not a warrior, I am a worrier. If there was a TV show called *Australian Ninja Worrier* I could be the champion.

That said, I do need to confess that sometimes in moments of stress I will talk to myself out loud to offer myself encouragement, and the most embarrassing part is that when I talk to myself I don't call myself Wil, I call myself Ando. Yep, Ando. Even worse, I will proclaim loudly, 'Come on, Ando!' (as opposed to 'Come on Anh Do', which is the show I pitched to the ABC that nearly got me banned permanently from the building). In the Before Times I would say, 'Come on, Ando,' and find a way to get through any situation. But now, no matter how hard I try to encourage myself, there is always another voice there to rebut my arguments and it is much better at arguing than I am.

'Come on, Ando, think positive!'

Think positive? As in positive to Covid? Positive to monkeypox? No, thank you, get out of here with all your positive thinking.

'Come on, Ando, just go for a walk!'

A walk? Are you serious? Walking involves going outdoors and that is where the mosquitoes are. Will you be happy when I am positive . . . to Japanese encephalitis?

'Come on, Ando, just breathe!'

Breathe? Breathe? BREATHE? Are you kidding me? Have you not learned anything? Breathing is the worst thing you can do. That is how the Covid gets in, that is how the bushfire smoke gets in, and by the way, if breathing worked then you wouldn't have to keep doing it.

7

LOCKDOWN

With the Melbourne International Comedy Festival cancelled, there were a lot of comedians with new jokes and nothing to do with them, so the streaming service Stan stepped in and decided to make a show called *Lockdown Comedy Festival*. Basically, the idea was that they would get comedians to film some of their material at home and then piece it together into a series of television specials.

Covid restrictions meant that crews couldn't be sent out to film the pieces, so instead they decided they would send out the equipment to the comedians with instructions on how to set it up and film your set.

Personally I think that should have been the show: watching a bunch of comedians trying to put together their own equipment.

Sure, some of the younger comedians have more tech literacy, but for me this was the biggest challenge of my comedy career. Not doing the jokes, but working out how to record them. I am someone who has spent a quarter of a century on stage, where the only piece of electrical equipment I have to deal with on a daily basis is a microphone, and even that they don't really trust me with. I remember one gig I did, when I couldn't get the microphone to work, and finally someone asked, 'Have you turned it on?' No, I hadn't turned it on, because I didn't even know there was an On button, because until this gig no-one had ever trusted me with a mic that had an On and Off button, because they assumed I wouldn't know how to turn it on. And it turns out they were absolutely correct.

When I do a stage show, if something goes wrong with the microphone they have a simple solution. They don't expect me to get out a screwdriver and start repairing it. They have a spare microphone by my feet and I just pick up that one and get back on with the show. I don't know what happens if the back-up microphone stops working too. I guess I just shout louder.

So setting up my own equipment was definitely going to be a challenge. Luckily I had some time and nothing else to do. Getting the equipment to me would be more difficult than for most, now that I was living in the country, so they arranged for it to be shipped to Mullumbimby, from where it would be driven down the winding road to my house and dumped outside.

The reason it had to be delivered to the roadside was so we could guarantee contactless delivery, but I will say that there is nothing more suspect than living in the middle of nowhere and then getting a huge amount of recording equipment delivered. I had to get it inside quickly before the neighbours could start speculating. 'Well, I guess someone is making a porno during lockdown. I wonder what they are going to call it? *Living in the Bush*? *The Groin Transfer*? He always puts his name in his shows, so what about *Free Willy* or *WILF*?'

I was the last act to film jokes for the Stan special. Technically I was the host of the final episode, so I needed to see what others had done so I could shoot some links. I discovered some of the more tech-literate comedians had used the equipment to make something more like a comedy sketch, or a short film. I admired their creativity; I am blown away by how talented the next generation is. They are awesome and doing great. That was not going to be me. The bad news is I have lots of limitations when it comes to comedy, but the good news is I am aware of what those limitations are. I just wanted to do a piece of stand-up straight down the camera. If I could do that I would be happy, because I knew that even that would be difficult without an audience. It's hard enough when there is an empty aisle down the middle of the room with no audience in it; this was going to be all aisle.

I hadn't really performed a show without an audience since my first season of the Melbourne International Comedy

Festival. The audience is what makes my job a job. Otherwise I am just a man spouting nonsense. My job is basically taking something people do for free every day—talk—and thinking I am good enough at this that people will pay to hear me. At the end of the day, it's only a job because the audience agrees it is, and if there is no audience, there is no job.

Yes, technically my show exists without the audience. I could write it down. I could recite it out loud to no-one or to the dogs, but to me it is not really a show until it is in front of an audience. That's why the experience for the comedian can be so different from night to night, even if the show is the same, because you are not really doing a show, you are playing the audience and every audience is different. The audience is my instrument, and the show is just what I use to play them. I don't play the guitar or the drums, I play the audience, although occasionally I do play drums on the head of an unsuspecting audience member.

The other way I sometimes think about it is that comedians are surfers and the audience is the ocean. It doesn't matter how good a surfer you may be, you need the ocean, and you have to adapt to the conditions. Sometimes it is going to be small waves, sometimes beautiful big ones, and sometimes it's really dangerous out there and there are sharks around. But if they take the ocean away entirely then you are just a person standing on a plank in the sand trying to hang ten.

I was more nervous than I wanted to admit about the idea of filming without an audience, so to make it a less intimidating experience for me we'd decided to set up a fake comedy club on the deck below the house. The thinking was, the more we could make it look and feel like the usual experience, the easier it would be for me to re-create it.

I found an old rug that had a circle in the middle that would look like a light was being shone on me. It had a small stain on it, but some Apple Cider Vinegar would get that right out. I had a microphone and stool we could use, and while there was no brick wall I had picked up some fake brick wallpaper at Spotlight (seemed appropriate), which I had stuck up randomly in the background. It looked pretty good. I mean, not the best club I had ever played, not purpose-built for comedy, but definitely a club I would play. Plus it was really close to home, which is always a bonus for me.

I set up the equipment using the instructions provided, and decided in consultation with the director that the best time to film with the natural light would be between 10 a.m. and 12 noon, which seemed like more than enough time to film seven minutes of stand-up. It was all set up and ready to go: it would only take seven minutes to shoot if I nailed it the first time. Maybe ten minutes, just to be safe. Most of the time when we film things for television, I will try to do only one take. This is not a tribute to my capacity to nail it the first time, more a condemnation of my capacity for improvement through repetition.

I got up early the next morning to prepare. I checked the charge on all the equipment, turned it off to conserve the battery, and decided it was time to get ready. The brief was to dress up in my normal show clothes, though it was hard to feel too normal doing comedy at ten o'clock on a Monday morning, which might be the least comedy time of all. Having done breakfast radio, I can tell you that even 6 a.m. is a funnier time than ten. I am not sure why, it just is. I had a coffee, jumped into the shower, put on my show clothes, and got ready for my gig.

The nerves were definitely there. I don't usually get nervous before a show anymore but this was something different. The main thing I was concerned about was forgetting my script. You might think it is weird to be worried about remembering seven minutes when my usual show goes for 70. But when I usually do my shows, they are not tightly scripted. I tend to have the gist of what I want to say, and then I like to see how it naturally comes out on the night.

I once asked the former Australian cricket captain Steve Waugh what it was like to face the West Indian bowlers. How did you make the decision what shot to play when a ball was coming at your face at 160 kilometres per hour? He told me that you didn't have time to decide. You just needed to train as well as you could, and then, when you were out there, trust your instincts that you will play the right shot. Try to get out of your own head and out of your own way. That is the approach I like to take with my stand-up. Part of the reason I normally like to keep my show a bit loose is that I have a theory that there are two distinct states of stand-up comedy: creation and *re*-creation. Creation is coming up with the idea, the joke, the wording, the first time you say it on stage, the first time you get a laugh. Creation has an energy all of its own and it's always been my favourite part of the process. I guess it's why I have always loved doing improvised shows so much, as they are constant creation and that feels like mainlining creative energy. When I am doing a fully improvised show, I think about it like jumping out of an aeroplane without a parachute and knowing that you have to learn how to fly on the way down. You also have to be comfortable that sometimes you are going to crash before you work it out, but that is the joy of creation. To put it another way, when I am doing my completely improvised shows I always promise the crowd '70 minutes of quality material no matter how long it takes'.

Re-creation, on the other hand, is when the jokes have been tested and you are trying to say it in a way that has worked most often, to re-create a night or moment when it worked well. I often say to people that if you want to see what I thought my show was going to be, you have to come on the first night. After that the show becomes what the audience and I agree it is. Re-creation is an important part of the process, but it has never been my favourite part, and I think—as well as lack of talent—it is the main reason I have never enjoyed acting. (Side note: I have only ever acted twice on television and they were both cameos in shows playing myself and I really don't think I nailed the role either time.)

As a performer I always feel most comfortable in the act of creation, so when I am touring I tend to keep my stand-up shows loose to keep the creative spirit engaged, and I try and feed off the audience's energy to create something unique to the evening and use the bits when they are laughing to think about what I am going to say next and how I am going to say it.

But for this show my ocean had been drained, and I was worried. My usual approach would not suit the circumstances. I knew I had to script exactly what I was going to say and then learn it word for word. So that is what I did.

8

EAR

I turned the cameras and recording equipment on, checked that every red light that needed to be on was on, and tested my microphone to make sure it was registering. Is this thing on? Yes, it is, good. Alright, it is time to do this. Come on, Ando.

I stood on my spot in the middle of the rug, took a deep breath and started to talk. Word after rehearsed word spilled out of my mouth and when I got to the end I realised that despite my doubts I had nailed it. First go. You would not believe it. I shouldn't have been nervous at all; it came out perfectly. Well, not perfectly, but as well as I could have hoped for in the circumstances. To the point where I thought, maybe I should have been doing this the whole time? Maybe I would be a much better comedian if I learned my material.

The only downside was that the set had run for more like eight minutes on the timer, but I was sure they could fix that in the edit. It was 10.15 a.m. and I was done. Not quite as quick as I had estimated, but only five minutes of overtime. I felt really proud of myself that I had overcome something that scared me and found a way to adapt. Maybe some real positive growth would come out of these hard times. I said out loud to myself, 'Well done, Ando, you are a warrior!' And then I felt embarrassed because I was still recording and that would now be on the end of the set, because I did not know how to edit it out. I decided I would just tell them to watch until the end of the set and then immediately turn it off.

I turned off the recorders and, as I had been advised, checked the tape. (That's how old I am: there was definitely not any tape.) As soon as I started watching, I realised the mistake I had made. Somehow, instead of my entire body being shot, I had managed to film eight minutes of a close-up of my ear. Shit. Good one, Ando.

If I was a hipper young comedian I might have sent it in like that and pretended it was what I wanted to do. Don't you understand I am making a statement about the fact that I want people to listen to what I am saying? That society would be better if we listened more instead of talking? Or, there is no audience but I can still hear you, or 'I Lobe You', or something?

I knew I couldn't send in eight minutes of my ear, so I had to film it again. It was fine: I had one hour and 45 minutes left in my window, so why not? I had nailed it once. How hard could it be to nail it again? Very hard, as it turned out. On

41

my second attempt, I got about five minutes through the set before I flubbed something and had to start again. The third attempt, I made it about four minutes in before I messed up. And by the fourth attempt, I could barely make it two minutes. The harder I tried, the worse it was going, and when on my fifth attempt I stumbled over the very first line I knew it was time for a break.

I was now halfway through my filming window and didn't have anything useable. My palms were sweaty and my mouth was dry and I needed a drink. And maybe I needed something a little stronger than the coffee I'd had before I started. Usually when I performed my stand-up, I would have an alcoholic drink. It was one of my favourite things about the job, that they let you drink while you are working.

They don't let you do that if you are a pilot. Although if the pilot slurred a little in his announcement, I think we would all pay a little more attention to where the emergency exits are and where they keep the lifejackets. You're not meant to operate heavy machinery when you are under the influence of alcohol, but they didn't even let me touch the microphone usually, so I should have been okay.

Seeing as I had nothing to do for the rest of the day, and by rest of the day I mean rest of the week, and by rest of the week I mean rest of the year (and little did I know most of the next year as well), I decided that I should have a drink. I went upstairs and grabbed a beer out of the fridge and drank it. I then grabbed another beer and put it in my coffee mug on the stage with me. My glass was half full, of coffee-flavoured beer.

I had 50 minutes left when I pressed record and started again. This attempt was better. I got about five minutes in, which was way more than I had on my last few attempts, so the obvious conclusion was that the beer had helped. I almost made it the entire way through, so clearly I just hadn't had enough beer. I finished the beer in my coffee cup and grabbed another. I drank that and pressed record and started again. This time it all came out in a row, and I was done with a full 20 minutes left to spare. I felt like I had learned some lessons, but they were all bad ones.

I also realised I was a little drunk on a Monday morning doing a show to no-one in my pretend comedy club, that there had only really been a couple of weeks of proper lockdown and I was already one of those people who don't tell their family they have lost their job and just get dressed every day and pretend to go to work and then sit in the park and sip vodka out of their briefcase. I am not fine, thanks.

9

HOLE

I hadn't been unemployed in a long time, and while in the next 24 months I was lucky enough to have a couple of short-term TV gigs that helped pay some bills, when it came to performing live I reached the point where I had cancelled or rescheduled more shows than I had actually done and so I just stopped planning shows. The only question now was: what would I do with my time?

I still had my podcasts that could happen online, but after we covered our costs making them they weren't providing an income. Most people know what a podcast is these days, but for those who don't it is basically an imaginary radio show. Just like a radio show, but the main difference is . . . you don't get paid for it. I had not one, not two, not three, but four different podcasts, which meant I had a whole imaginary radio station to occupy me. But I couldn't pay my real bills in imaginary dollars.

One day it occurred to me: shit, I might have to get another job. That scared me because after a quarter of a century telling dick jokes to strangers in bars it turns out I don't have a whole lot of transferable skills.

I do have a journalism degree, but I hadn't used that since I started doing stand-up and it had never been relevant to that job. You don't need a degree to be a comedian. I have had a lot of heckles over the years but no-one has ever yelled out, 'Show us your qualifications!'

I don't think I would have the skills to go back to being a journalist, although to be fair these days apparently all you need is an iPhone and you can declare yourself an independent journalist. And I did have an iPhone. I also had an iPad. I worried I might be overqualified. But if you can just declare yourself something, why would I aim for something as low as journalism? Screw that, I would declare myself an independent doctor. After all, I haven't done journalism for 25 years, but I have self-medicated consistently.

I racked my brain, but without comedy I couldn't think of a way I could meaningfully contribute to the world. I didn't know how I felt about that, but I knew it wasn't fine.

I tried to remember back to when I had the potential to contribute something to the world. I had to go back a long way. I had to go all the way back to high school where in Year 11 I had received a report card saying, 'Wil is easily distracted but capable of so much if he would just apply himself a little harder and not try to be funny all the time.' That's a lot to unpack, but at the time I didn't unpack it at all. All I thought was, people think I am funny? That's cool. Then I didn't really read the rest because I got distracted by the funny thing, so I guess my teacher was right about that.

Who was that teacher? What was that potential they saw in me? I really wish I knew now what they thought they knew then. I wish I had asked them. I wondered if it would be weird for me to track them down and ask, 'Hey, do you remember 30-odd years ago when you thought I had potential? I have some follow-up questions. What did you see in me? What is it that you think I was capable of? Because I am looking for some suggestions.'

One thing I did not consider was politics. That is definitely not for me. I don't feel like I can run my own life particularly effectively, so I am certainly not looking to enshrine my dumb opinions in legislation. But it did come up when war started in Ukraine, where the leader of the country was a former comedian who had played the president of Ukraine on a TV comedy and people liked him so much he was now the president.

When people in Australia first heard about this, there was a certain section of the community that got very excited. They remembered that Shaun Micallef had played the prime minister on a comedy show on television, and that meant that maybe Shaun Micallef could be the prime minister of

Australia. They thought that was a very good idea, and don't get me wrong, I think it is a great idea too, but there is no way that Shaun Micallef would be elected prime minister in Australia. Shaun is too good for us as a nation. We don't deserve Shaun.

Yes, he would scoop the inner-city ABC-watching audience, but then the votes would come in from Far North Queensland and regional Western Australia and the new prime minister of Australia would be Kevin Bloody Wilson because he promised he would change the national anthem to 'Rooting In The Back Of A Ute' and now we're in a war with New Zealand because our prime minister asked Jacinda Ardern if she fucks on first dates.

Without an audience to play, what skills did I have left? What could I contribute to the community? What was I even good at? Until 2020 I had written and performed at least one new stand-up show a year for 25 years. That was more than half of my life. For a quarter of a century I had trained my brain to look at my life and the world and then process my thoughts about them into a show. When the pandemic hit there were no more shows, but that part of my brain didn't turn off. It turned in. It turned on myself.

I remember in the early days of the pandemic I would hear from some friends who were actually enjoying not working and were bingeing TV series. I was jealous when I heard that. I hadn't been bingeing TV. I had been bingeing every decision I had made in my life until that point. They say your life flashes before your eyes when you die; well, I had a version of that during the pandemic. My brain replayed everything I had done and, I have to say, some seasons of that series were hard viewing. There were times when I really didn't like the star of the show. Is he meant to be the hero of this story? He is not awesome and he is not doing great. I hope he gets recast.

I think the main thing I lost was a sense of certainty. I know this sense was always artificial, but the artifice had been shattered in my mind in a way that I am not sure it will ever be rebuilt. I find it amazing now when I meet anyone who is certain about anything anymore. I love the optimism of people who make long-term plans. Personally I find it hard to lock in a plan unless that plan is for later in the day, and even then I assume it's 50/50 at best, and the odds are only that strong if the plan is to do something later in the day in my own house.

The unexpectedly tough thing for me was losing my sense of time. Comedy is so much about timing, but it is also about time. You have to know how to be funny for five minutes, seven minutes, ten minutes, half an hour, an hour, two hours. And you need to know what those times feel like. I don't know what time feels like anymore. All the events in my life seem jumbled together; sometimes a minute feels like a year and a month feels like a second, like everything and nothing are happening all at once. I am at the point where if I woke up one day and a murderer had scrawled on the window,

'I know what you did last summer', I would be grateful. I would reply, 'What did I do? Please talk me through it because I have no idea. For starters, what is summer?'

The loss of a sense of time started to infect my dreams, and then for a while things got a little darker than that. For about a month, every night when I went to bed I would have dreams about how I would die. That was troubling enough, but the thing that really disturbed me was the feeling I would have when I died: relief.

I was clearly not fine, but there was still something funny about my death dreams, because in every single one I would die peacefully in bed. No matter the scenario, the one constant was that my death would happen peacefully in bed. Sometimes I would already be in bed, but sometimes it would be the most fantastical situation, like a battle on a pirate ship, and I would survive the bloodied battle and then go downstairs to bed and die peacefully in my sleep.

After about four weeks of this, my dreams took a darker turn again. This time I still died in my bed, but I was murdered. Even worse, my murder was unsolved. But it didn't stop there. Eventually my unsolved murder became the subject of a true crime podcast and it became the biggest podcast in the world, and while it didn't solve my murder it did mean I had finally found a way to make some money out of podcasting. The saddest thing of all about this story is that even in my death ideation dreams I was still thinking about content.

I knew I probably needed to talk to a professional, but I had just moved house and was between therapists and it turns out the peak of a global pandemic is not a good time to be looking for a new one. Turns out they are a bit busy. When the world has gone through a collective trauma, there is a long waiting list for professional therapists, and even the unprofessional ones are pretty busy.

In Mullumbimby, the waiting list at most places was about a year, which is ideal when it comes to therapy. 'What's that? You have some problems you need to deal with now? What I recommend is you let them really fester for a year. That way, when you do eventually get in for therapy, you will really get your money's worth. That is what we call a glass-half-full way of looking at it. Plus, the way the world is going, in 365 days so many more bad things are going to happen. You won't even want to talk about Covid anymore once those flesh-eating aliens arrive.'

I secretly suspect the reason there is such a long waiting list for therapists is that they are all too busy talking each other through this. It must have been such an incredibly tough time for those who were dealing with their own world changing while they had to help their patients deal with theirs. 'You should have heard the shit this guy said to me today . . . and all I did was ask him how he was. He kept banging on about some winding road that he thought was trying to kill him and then he talked about being murdered in his dream and it being turned into a podcast. Then he just kept muttering, "Content, content, content" over and over until the end of the session. I don't know what is wrong with him, but he is not fine.'

The break from doing shows did have an upside. Not constantly travelling and sleeping each night in an unfamiliar bed saw a marked improvement in my pain levels from my back and hips. I have had osteoarthritis in my hips for over fifteen years, and in the last couple of years had been suffering from some crippling hip-related back injuries as well. It quickly became clear that the thing I loved the most was also the thing that was killing me and that if your body is a temple, I had been treating mine more like a hotel room. You might respect it, but if someone else is going to wash the sheets, you don't mind eating in bed.

It probably also helped that I had moved to a warmer climate than I had been used to. There is a reason that older people move to places where the weather is warmer for the aches in their bones. It actually works. I guess that is the only good thing I can see when it comes to climate change. I might have to fight in the climate wars, but at least my hips won't hurt as much while I am fighting.

The other thing was that I stopped drinking alcohol. I didn't mean to. It just kinda happened. I realised that I used to only drink when I was at work, and I used to work a lot. When the work went away, so did the drinking, and one day I just stopped completely and my hips felt better. I shouldn't have been surprised. I had been told for years that drinking was bad for arthritis and inflammation, but it was one of those things that I ignored because . . . well, because I didn't want it to be true.

My back pain disappeared completely, which was incredible because I had been suffering for years with a chronic bad back. When you hurt your back, you find people ask you the same question: 'How did you hurt your back?' And from that question you immediately know something about that person: they are under the age of 40, because if you're under 40 you still live in a world where you think that all injuries have *explanations*.

Young people are always complaining, 'The world is a tyre fire. There's climate change, disease and I will never be able to afford a house.' All that is terrible, young people, I agree, and I hope we can help fix some of it for you, but I also need you to know that the other day I sneezed and my elbow fell off.

You want to know how I hurt my back? Here's how I hurt my back. I went to sleep one night and my back was fine, and I woke up the next morning and my back was fucked. Apparently I strained my back during a particularly vigorous dream. Must have been that pirate fight. The upside is if my back was hurting this much in my dream, I would be glad if someone murdered me. It's not a very cool way to do yourself an injury. I don't think Martin Luther King would have been so revered if his speech had been: 'I had a dream . . . and I think I slipped a disc!'

(I told a version of that joke on the Gold Coast one night and literally no-one laughed. It was so silent in the room that a girl was whispering to her friend but everyone heard her. She said, 'Who is Martin Luther King?' And then someone else replied, 'Some kind of king I reckon?' And then another person said, 'What, like Wally Lewis?' True story. Sometimes I play the audience, and sometimes they are playing with themselves.)

At one stage my back was so bad I literally couldn't sit down for three months. I could stand up, which is handy as I am a stand-up comedian, and I could lie down, which is handy because I am a lay-down sleeper. But if I wanted to do anything in between I needed to be heavily medicated, and not in the fun way I usually like to be heavily medicated. I have always believed that drugs are wasted on the sick.

The problem with not being able to sit was that I occasionally host a TV panel show about advertising on the ABC, where the minimum requirement for the job is being able to sit down at the panel. So we needed to come up with a plan. One of the early suggestions was to raise the height of the desk we normally sat at to be more like a standing desk and everyone else on the panel could just stand up too. It would be good for everyone's backs! That seemed like a good plan until one day someone asked, 'Hey, do you think it's a problem that Wil is the tallest person on the show, so if we set the desk at the correct height for him, everyone else will be under the desk?' Yes, I think it will be a problem if Todd

Sampson is under the desk; for starters the viewers won't be able to see his t-shirt.

The next suggestion was even more creative. The idea was that everyone else would sit at the desk like normal, but where my chair would usually be they would just dig a hole. Yes, you read that right. Dig a hole, or, as it is known in Australia, the Dale Kerrigan solution. They weren't joking. Their plan was to dig a hole and then I could just get dressed in my suit and stand in the hole at desk height and no-one would know that I was standing in a hole. Someone actually said that to me in a meeting. I said, 'I think they will spot that I am standing in a hole.' But they were clearly prepared for this, because they said, 'No, we've thought of that. What we are going to do is get the props department to sticky-tape a fake chair to your back.'

The trickiest thing to handle with the bad back was the show schedule. Because I couldn't sit, I couldn't drive or catch a taxi or Uber, so, in order to stand the whole way, every day I had to catch two buses and a train to work. It took two hours each way and messed up everyone else's day. The pain in my back was a pain in everyone else's arse.

The ABC literally considered hiring me a stretch limousine to go to and from work every day. Your taxpayer dollars at work. But their plan wasn't that I would lie down comfortably in the back. No, their plan was that they would get one with a sunroof. And I would stand with my head out of the sunroof on the way to work. Of course. Now that is fine if you are the Pope going to work. Or if you are at Schoolies Week on the Gold Coast or Richard Gere at the end of *Pretty Woman*. But can you imagine going to work this way every day in the city at peak hour? 'Hello! Hey, how you doing? Yep, just an ordinary guy going to work in a totally normal way. You can tell how normal this is from this chair that I have taped to my back.'

10

WEED

The main thing that brought me relief from my pain was medicinal cannabis. Who would have guessed the solution to joint pain was there in the name all along? My pain is chronic and so is the weed that I use to treat it. I am on the government medicinal cannabis program. I have a specialist cannabis doctor. He is a real doctor. His name is Dre, Dr Dre. He's straight outta Compton (Medical University). Some motherfuckers act like they forgot about him, but I didn't. So anyway, Dr Dre said . . . nothing, you idiots. Dr Dre's dead, he's locked in my basement.

I was actually the first person from the Northern Rivers of New South Wales to be accepted into the medicinal cannabis program. I know this because the official I was talking to when I was registering said, 'You are the first person from the Northern Rivers who has accessed this program.'

I replied, 'Good sir, that is counterintuitive to what I know about the place I have chosen to live in.'

He paused and said something that was so true it made me laugh out loud. 'Mate, I reckon they might be sorted!'

Yes, sir, I think you might be right.

It does mean that I can now travel with my medicine from state to state when I tour, which has been great news for me and terrible news for 'small business people' I had been supporting as I moved around the country. Tough end of financial year for some local weed dealers.

Before I used cannabis medicinally I used it recreationally, although I think that even then I was self-medicating. I should point out again, I am not a doctor, not even an 'independent doctor', but I have appeared on television, which I think qualifies you to dispense medical advice these days.

I came to weed late. I didn't try it properly until I was in my thirties. In my opinion that seems like the right time to try it. I think if alcohol is legal at eighteen they should make weed legal for everyone at 30. But not before then. If you try it too early in life it can mess with your brain, and we know that it's not always great for motivation. It is good to build something first and then find weed when you need to chill out a bit.

I first used medicinal cannabis when I was living in Los Angeles. I was based there six months a year doing shows all over the US. Over nearly a decade I performed in more than half the US states. It's fair to say the medicinal cannabis system there was nowhere near as strict as in Australia. When I went to my first appointment, I arrived at the doctor's office with my X-rays and my referrals and the doctor almost laughed, he was so relieved. He explained that the majority of his day was spent coaching stoners through the interview to find something that would result in them walking out of that office with a cannabis card. He said, 'Oh, you really qualify for this program. This saves me so much time!' Apparently the consultation could often last for 45 minutes until they finally found the 'reason' the stoner qualified for the card. I probably should have known from the fake brick wallpaper in the doctor's office. You got that at Spotlight, didn't you?

In Australia the range of cannabis products available is still pretty small, but that was not the case in the US. Any food or drink you could think of, they had probably tried to put cannabis in it. If there was a medicated Apple Cider Vinegar they may have invented the best product in the world.

There could be some dangers with the edibles, though. When cannabis was fully legalised, I had a friend stay with me who wanted to try it. He decided that he fancied some medicated caramel popcorn. It was delicious, but it also had a downside. You see, one of the best-known side-effects of weed is that it can make you hungry. And when you have the munchies, you know what sounds really delicious? Caramel popcorn. And so you have some more of that, and you get the munchies so you want some more caramel popcorn, and then you get the munchies and this cycle only stops when there is no more caramel popcorn and you go to the fridge to try to find some product that *isn't* infused with cannabis.

Eventually I needed to go to bed, but when I was drifting off to sleep I could hear my friend banging around the rest of the house. It started in the bathroom, but moved through the small apartment. It sounded like he was opening every cupboard in every room. Then I heard him open the fridge and the freezer. I assumed that he was looking for something to eat so I went to sleep.

The next day, after a very deep sleep, over breakfast and coffee I asked him what he had been doing the night before. He explained that he had misplaced his sleep apnoea device, which is something you can probably pick up from the name that he wears to sleep. And it's pretty important because it keeps him from dying in his sleep. And although I am not a doctor, I can tell you that dying in your sleep is bad for your health. Though at least it's a nice way to go, much better than dying in a misguided pirate fight on the high seas. (Side note: I assume the seas were so high to treat their chronic pain.)

The sleep apnoea device is not a little mouthguard. It is more like what they would strap Hannibal Lecter into for an interview. Anyway, my friend couldn't find it. So he looked in the obvious places. And then, as you do, he started looking in the non-obvious places. He knew there was no way it wasn't in the apartment. But you know you are desperate when you are checking inside the freezer and the washing machine. Maybe I dropped it in there when I was doing my laundry. Anyway, it was only when he went into the bathroom and looked in the mirror that he realised his mistake. He had been wearing it the whole time. So yeah, edibles can be dangerous.

Because of this I want to always be responsible in my use of my medicine, especially when driving. In the US they have impairment tests, but in Australia our road laws are behind when it comes to medicinal cannabis. Our tests only show whether it is still in your system and not whether you are impaired. And it can stay in your system for a long time after you are no longer impaired. Which is not great when it comes to a medicine that you have to use every day for your pain. I didn't want to give up driving, but I also didn't want to put anyone in danger, so I went to my doctor and asked him.

He said, 'The latest research suggests it impairs you for about two hours, but what I recommend to be safe is if you have to drive anywhere, use the medicine the night before and sleep it off and then do all the driving you need to do the next day before you use it again and you should have no risk of being impaired. But there is a small chance that if you haven't brushed your teeth properly and you get pulled over for a random drug test, you still might report a positive.'

Well, this was bad news. 'So what am I supposed to do?'

'Well, what I recommend is in your glovebox you keep a bottle of Apple Cider Vinegar. What you do is swirl it around in your mouth and it will fool the machine.' And all I could think was, they've got to you too, Doc. I see what is happening here. This is the work of Big Apple Cider Vinegar. I can smell it on your breath.

11

HIGH

When I was in the US in 2014, I got invited onto *Getting Doug with High*, a chat show hosted by comedian Doug Benson. It is a regular interview show but instead of sipping drinks like they might on *The Graham Norton Show*, they smoke marijuana. As you can imagine, as the show goes on the conversation becomes more and more loose. It has featured names like Jack Black, Kevin Smith, Dan Harmon, David Cross, Craig Robinson, Sarah Silverman, Aubrey Plaza, Tiffany Haddish, and Abbi Jacobson and Ilana Glazer from *Broad City*. They had even had the original stoners, Cheech & Chong, as guests.

I definitely wanted to do the show. But I had a couple of issues. The first was I wanted to make sure that it was legal for me. When you are an immigrant working on a visa in another country, you want to make sure everything you do is legitimate. And I was interested in what the reaction would be in Australia, where what I was doing wasn't legal. I definitely didn't want to have any trouble getting back in, although it would be ironic if they didn't let someone into Australia because they committed a crime, seeing as that's the whole way the modern country was founded.

The first one I checked off simply. I would be a person doing a legal thing in a place where it was legal, which is the very definition of something not being against the law.

The second one, it turned out, was more of an issue. The major tabloid newspaper chain in Australia decided to make a big deal of it, not I think because they had an actual problem with it but because I work occasionally for the national broadcaster and they wanted to beat up on them. If they needed some ammunition, I should have leaked the story that the ABC planned to hire me a stretch limousine and have me host the show from inside a hole.

The tabloids wanted a tabloid-style scandal, so they published photos of me smoking on the show as if they were leaked pictures, not something from a show that was broadcast and is still available to watch online. They even tried to pressure my employers to sack me. Luckily it turned out that doing something legal in a place where it was legal wasn't a ground for sacking someone.

I found out the story was going to be running in the paper the next day when the reporter contacted me for a quote. I didn't supply one, but I did know that it meant one thing:

I would have to call Mum. If there are going to be photos of you smoking weed running in the most popular paper in the country, I think it is polite to give your parents a heads-up about it. That's not something you just want them to discover in the paper over their breakfast.

The other thing that I knew was that I was probably going to be asked a lot of questions online the next day. As someone who has been through a couple of scandals in his life, I've found that sometimes the best thing to do is to step away from social media for a few days and wait for it to pass. But on this issue, I felt like I had nothing to be ashamed of, and decided that if anyone messaged me in good faith, even if they had a problem with what I did, I would try to answer them in good faith too.

The time difference between LA and Australia meant that I had time to get up in the morning and read the story before most people in Australia had woken up. Of course the piece was deliberately inflammatory, so I waited for the criticism to come. And I waited. And then I waited some more. And then I waited some more. But it never came. In fact, despite what the article was trying to achieve, I never had one single person contact me to criticise me for my appearance on the show.

What I did get was hundreds of messages of support. Hundreds. People thanking me for being a public advocate for them. (I hadn't been intending this, but that was how they received it.) And I got some questions. In fact, I got a lot of questions. Most of them were from people who suffered from chronic pain like me and wanted to know if medicinal cannabis would be good for them. As usual I pointed out that I was not a doctor, but was happy to answer their questions to the best of my ability.

One message I got was from a lady who was in her eighties and was in severe pain but nothing was working. Cannabis had been suggested but she didn't want to take it because it was against the law. I am not an expert, independent doctor's credentials aside, but that is cruel. Once you get to 70 you should be able to try whatever you want. You certainly should be able to smoke pot. That is the perfect time. You are responsible. You can sit around and eat biscuits. You can bake and get baked. You're already a bit forgetful so no-one will notice.

In the end there was no downside to the media coverage. There was only upside. I got to help some people find some relief for their pain, and it also meant that for a couple of years after that story ran, everywhere I went in public someone would sidle up to me and offer me a joint. I didn't always take them up on the offer, but it was nice to be asked. Anyway, that is the story about the time the biggest media organisation in the country thought they were going to do a hit piece on me to destroy my life, and instead basically put a full-page ad in their paper that said, 'This is Wil Anderson. If you see him, please offer him some weed! Call him Cypress Wil.'

12

FIRE

I feel incredibly bad for younger Australians who may never be able to afford a house, but I have a tip if you are looking for a discount on one: buy it when the area is in the middle of a bushfire.

Nothing brings excitement to your life quite like signing the contract on the Wednesday before the Thursday when there is an evacuation order for the area because they think it might burn down.

At least when the 2019–20 bushfires were happening I was in the country, unlike the prime minister, Scott Morrison, who was in Hawaii. To be fair, the prime minister said that in hindsight he wouldn't have gone. The problem with that excuse was that the country was already on fire before he left. He didn't need hindsight, he just needed actual sight. He needed to look out the window as he took off to Honolulu and think, hang on, that place I am in charge of is on fire!

You know you've messed up as prime minister when you get zinged by Lara Bingle. In his former life Morrison was in charge of the model's famous tourism campaign. Now, in a time of national crisis, Bingle tweeted, 'Hey Scott Morrison . . . where the bloody hell are you?' Take that. More like Lara ZINGle. (Lara We're Not Worthyington.) They later arrested her for burning the prime minister like that on a total-fire-ban day.

There are some leaders who aspire to the job because when the shit hits the fan they think they are the person best qualified to coordinate the clean-up and order a new fan. Then there was our prime minister. While our country was on fire, our PM was in Hawaii. He had once launched a major tourism campaign asking people to holiday in Australia, and now he was pissing off to Honolulu. He later said, 'We normally holiday on the South Coast but we couldn't go there because it was on fucking fire.' That may not have been exactly what he said, but that's what I heard.

My favourite part of his excuse was that he wanted to get back but it was hard to get a flight. Hang on, it's Honolulu, not Haiti. He would be terrible on *The Amazing Race*. Also, when someone says *The Amazing Race*, he thinks they are talking about white people. 'It's hard to get a flight' might be an acceptable excuse if you were not the prime minister of Australia. I think they would let you sit in the cockpit, which, after all, is named after YOU.

He also famously said, 'I don't hold a hose.' Which surprised me, because he looked like a massive hose holder. And even though he doesn't hold a hose, I bet he could grab one out of a volunteer's hand against their will. Do you remember that handshake? Bernie from *Weekend at Bernie's* shakes hands more enthusiastically than that volunteer firefighter. It was like Morrison was shaking hands with a muppet. Except that he was the muppet.

The problem was, their tragedy was his photo opportunity. One firefighter told him he hadn't eaten all day. At this the PM's brain went through all the possible responses and landed on, 'Well, I'll let you get back to it!'

I'll. Let. You. Get. Back. To. It. How about you fuck off back to Hawaii, mate. Oh yeah, must be on a diet. He's doing intermittent fasting. The 5:2. I get it. Gives you clarity. Must be looking forward to CHEAT DAY!

The bushfires weren't just happening at my new home. They were happening near my old home too. Where I grew up, in East Gippsland, Victoria, the entire town of Mallacoota was evacuated by boat. That's pretty shocking, seeing an entire town getting onto boats. And even worse, the home affairs minister at the time, Peter Dutton, saw the boats and sent them all to Christmas Island. That is his solution for everything: send them to Christmas Island. Refugees, Christmas Island. Coronavirus, Christmas Island. Too much stuff in the shed, Christmas Island. Last year's Christmas tree: Christmas Island.

I went to school with a guy from Mallacoota who had the best high school nickname of all time. He was called the Mallacoota Rooter. I don't know if he came up with it, but I know he was proud of it. I didn't realise how attached I was to that nickname until the fires in Mallacoota. I was watching the news and was so shocked I said out loud, 'I hope The Rooter is okay!' That is a weird thing to say out of context when you are watching footage of people being evacuated. For all I knew, some of those kids could have been his. Maybe all of them.

They had to send in the navy to evacuate people from Mallacoota. My favourite part of the story is that the people of Mallacoota said, 'If you're coming anyway, can you bring some beer? Some travellers?' They got the navy to deliver 3000 litres of beer. Now that is a booze cruise. Five-star service from a four-star admiral. *'In the navy, you can sail the seven seas. In the navy, you can deliver some VBs.'*

It's hard to remember now, so much has happened since, but it wasn't that long ago we were all wearing masks not for Covid, but for smoke. There was so much smoke in the summer of 2019–20 they said that going outside for a jog was the equivalent of smoking 50 cigarettes. So finally, by staying inside and not going for a jog, I was technically on a health kick. In fact, you could smoke three bongs and as long as you didn't open the window that was still the healthy option. Again, I am legally obliged to point out that this is not medical advice and I am not a doctor.

There were people who were still jogging in the smoke, which seemed counterproductive to me. The only time you should run in the smoke is if you are being chased by a fire. When you are running in the smoke it's not healthy anymore. That is like thinking the end of *Shawshank* involved Andy Dufresne going for a healthy swim.

One of the side-effects of smoking too much pot is it makes your lungs like leather, which is normally not something to be proud of, but suddenly it was a superpower. When I did have to go outside in the smoke, I found it didn't affect me as much as others. One day I was walking up a hill and something amazing happened—I passed a jogger. All that training for *Getting Doug* really helped. This was a miracle, as I barely passed any joggers when I used to be able to jog.

But since I have had osteoarthritis in my hips, I haven't experienced anything like that. The rush of adrenaline was amazing. What had happened was, this man was jogging in the smoke, and his healthy lungs couldn't hack it. He had kept them too healthy and pristine and it was too much too fast, whereas the inside of my lungs looked like Tommy Lee Jones's face. I walked by this jogger who was having a coughing fit with his hands on his knees. It was amazing. I felt powerful. I whispered, 'You gotta cough to get off!'

So I guess what I am saying is that I think that pot smokers are the next evolution of humanity. 'We did it, we're in charge now! Time to get Insane in the Membrane!'

Whether it is fires or floods, every time there is a natural disaster in Australia, there is one thing that you are bound to hear from those who want to deny the impacts of climate change. 'Well, this is nothing new, this has happened before. We have always had floods and fires and droughts.'

Yes, we have always had those things, but I am not sure that 'This has happened before' is the compelling argument you think it is. Yes, it has happened before, but the more compelling issue is that it is happening right now, and chances are it's going to happen again soon, and worse. Here's an idea: when things have happened before, let's learn from that and try not to have them happen again?

At the very least, stop saying it while the natural disaster is still happening. Surprisingly, when someone is going through the trauma of losing their home and possessions—and sometimes loved ones—the amazing revelation that it has happened before isn't much of a comfort to them. 'I have nowhere to live and have lost everything I owned and cared about, but now that I know this has happened before, I suppose I mustn't grumble!'

Yes, I know your grandpa is dead but grandparents have died before, so wipe those tears away and get on with things. Try to see the glass as half full: you are going to save money on Christmas presents this year.

It's like when someone tries to deny global warming by saying, 'I remember it being hotter!' Yeah, well I remember *The Goodies* being a great show but have you ever tried to rewatch it? Sometimes things aren't exactly how we remember them. Just because your grandma remembers it being hotter one day when she was young doesn't mean we should shut down the Bureau of Meteorology. I'll trust scientific records over your nan's memory.

Even worse is when politicians bring up The Poem. Much like Godwin's Law, which states that the longer an internet debate goes on, the more likely someone will compare something to Hitler, in Australia we have Dorothea's Law, which states that the longer a debate goes on about the cause of natural disasters, the more likely a politician will bring up that fucking poem.

For those who don't know what I'm talking about, the poem in question is called 'My Country', by Dorothea Mackellar, and the most famous—and most quoted by politicians—verse reads: 'I love a sunburnt country, / A land of sweeping plains, / Of ragged mountain ranges, / Of droughts and flooding rains.'

Climate-change-denying politicians love to use this poem as proof that Australia has always had natural disasters and that fossil fuels have nothing to do with what we are currently experiencing. Also, it is just coincidence that these politicians take large donations from these fossil fuel companies. But again, I should point out that that is not the reason they deny climate science; it's the poem, the sacred poem.

What I love about politicians quoting this poem is how most of the politicians who do are the type who usually loathe the arts. Normally they would think poets were a bunch of pot-smoking dole bludgers (whereas that's more your stand-up comedians), but if you happen to have written something that suggests we have previously had floods and droughts then they will quote you until the end of time. If you can rhyme 'hero' and 'net zero', they might make you the poet laureate. The next time a pollie is being asked about natural disasters in Australia and they quote this poem, the follow-up question from the journalist should be, 'Before we go on, name one other poem!' I am sure there would be one politician who replied, 'Well, I know one about a boy standing on a burning bridge with his pockets full of crackers, but before I tell it I need to point out that the bridge fire was not caused by climate change and bridges have caught fire before.'

I should point out that my problem is not with the poem itself. It's a great poem, filled with powerful imagery, written by Dorothea when she was only nineteen and living in England, and according to legend might have been finished when she was on holiday in Hawaii. (Knowing that, it's surprising the former prime minister didn't learn a version of it on the ukulele.) It's a great poem, and the reason it is a great poem is that it was written by a poet, and not a climate scientist. It's the same reason they get scientists and not poets to write the Intergovernmental Panel on Climate Change reports. Although maybe people would pay more attention if these rhymed: 'It's time to end fossil-fuelled insanity / Climate change is Code Red for humanity!'

13

VOLUNTEERS

If there is one upside to natural disasters it's seeing communities work together. I am always awed by volunteers and the sacrifices they make in times of crisis. During the bushfires, I was at an airport when I spotted some volunteer firefighters who were in transit to go and help out their mates interstate. They were lining up for their plane and I suddenly had the overwhelming urge to go and shake their hands and thank them.

But somehow that didn't seem like enough. I wanted to do something for them. I didn't want to give them money. Giving cash to a bunch of people dressed as firefighters felt too Magic Mike and not the tone I was going for. So instead I thought, I know they get hungry out there and don't have enough snacks. Some of them haven't eaten all day. I am going to buy them all the snacks I can afford. Forget *Snakes on a Plane*; this was going to be Snacks on a Plane.

The nearest snack shop was at the other end of the terminal, but they hadn't started boarding yet so I had some time. I found the place and went in and bought about $300 worth of assorted chocolates and lollies. It was so much fun, I felt like I was in Willy Wonka's chocolate factory, without all the weird child murder.

I don't think anyone had ever bought that many snacks in that shop at one time, because the woman working behind the counter was staring at me with a look that seemed to ask, 'How long is your flight? Are you just going to eat all these and run interstate?' Or: 'I guess we know who just had to swallow their stash to get through security.'

You might think it would be easy to buy $300 of sweets, but you don't live inside my head. Suddenly I realised that there were some choices that didn't seem very appropriate to give to a volunteer firefighter. Redskins, Caramello Koalas and snakes all seemed in bad taste. Fantales are no good because the firefighters won't have time to read the trivia, and the first Snickers bars I found had the labels Sleepy, Grouchy and Princess. No thank you. I eventually settled on Life Savers and Minties. It's moments like these you need Minties. I also bought lots of M&Ms because they melt in your mouth, not in your pocket while you are fighting fires. There were protein balls there but I refused to get them. Protein balls are not a present. That is like giving an educational toy for Christmas. Plus, you don't need unexpected gas near all that open flame.

I paid for my two shopping bags full of treats and staggered out of the shop. I looked like I was coming home from the Royal Agricultural Show, or I'd mugged a bunch of kids on Halloween. I realised I'd probably spent more time picking my snacks than I should have, so I started rushing towards the gate—and if you have never seen a man with osteoarthritis in his hips try to run while carrying two huge bags of chocolate, yes, it is exactly as graceful as you are imagining.

I started to sweat as I got closer to the gate, partly from the shuffling, partly the extra weight, and partly the sugar sweats from the couple of Caramello Koalas I had bought for myself and scoffed in the store. The sweat really started to pour when I couldn't see a line anymore at the gate. When I got there I realised that everyone had boarded the plane, and while it hadn't taken off yet, they had closed the gate.

I now felt like I was in a romantic comedy and the love of my life had just boarded the plane before I could declare my love to them. In the movies, they always convince the flight attendants to open the doors and let them on board, but I didn't think I could mount the argument: 'Stop the plane! I want to give them some choccies!'

So now I was left with $300 worth of chocolate bars and lollies. I did consider giving them out to children at the airport, but I realised that a sweaty middle-aged man standing around the carousel handing candy to children was probably not a great look. So instead I took them home and ate them myself. I guess I am the real hero, and definitely not the net zero.

14

WIGGLES

In times of trouble, the entertainment industry is among the first to offer our help. During the 2019–20 bushfires I was involved in a few fundraising shows, including a giant comedy gala at the Palais Theatre in Melbourne with all proceeds going to those most in need. But the best fundraising gig, without a doubt, was a show that will go down in show business history as one of the greatest live performances of all time. Of course, I am talking about The Wiggles.

To raise funds for bushfire relief, the original line-up of children's entertainment group The Wiggles re-formed to do a show. So this is already a great gig. It is for a good cause, and it is the original Wiggles getting back together. But the question that fascinated me was: who is that gig for? Who are the audience in the room? Because it is not kids, right? This is not a gig for children. They would be confused by this line-up of The Wiggles. They would ask their parents all sorts of questions like: why is Emma an old man now? These are not their Wiggles. That is not entertainment for them. That is a scenario you warn your kids about. A bunch of old men dressed up like The Wiggles trying to lure you into their Big Red Van? No, thank you. Here is our new song: 'Stranger Danger, Stranger Danger! Safety House, Safety House.'

So that means that the audience would actually be adults. I loved this idea. A Wiggles gig for a roomful of people who had literally grown up with these songs and now wanted to join together to rediscover the kid inside them. Consider that community, think about how incredible the energy would have already been in that room, plus the whole thing was happening to raise money for a great cause, so on that alone it would have been one of the greatest gigs of the year.

But that was not all that happened. Right towards the end of the show, Greg, the Yellow Wiggle, dropped dead on stage. Now, before anyone panics, he got better. He is fine now. I wouldn't be telling this story if he wasn't back up and Wiggling as well as ever. But die he did. At the end of their set, the Yellow Wiggle dropped to the floor. Everyone immediately gathered around and shouted, 'Wake up, Greg!' except for Jeff, who was really mad that Greg was stealing his bit.

I'm not lying when I say this was one of the great gigs of all time. You go and see your childhood heroes, the vibe in the room is amazing, and then at the end of the show one of them collapses on stage and dies. This is compelling.

What will happen next? Well, what happened next is the rest of The Wiggles went back on stage and did another song. You see, they didn't know that Greg was dying, they just thought he had collapsed from exhaustion and they should go back on stage to reassure the crowd. I get that logic—the show must go on—but it did mean that while Greg was in the wings dying, the last thing he would have been hearing was his friends singing 'Hot Potato, Hot Potato'. Move over Woodstock or Coachella, this is now the most legendary gig of all time.

But it was not done yet, because this wouldn't have been such a great show if Greg hadn't made it. If there had been a yellow coffin in the Big Red Hearse then this would not be a fun story, but the best is yet to come.

Greg died three times that night, but his life was actually saved by one of his fans. There was an off-duty nurse in the audience who jumped up on stage and used the defibrillator three times to bring him back to life. (The rest of the crew had been hopeless, as they only do CPR with their Wiggly fingers and that is not the correct method.)

When I think of this gig, and I do more often than you would imagine, I love to think of it from the nurse's perspective. Imagine you were a Wiggles fan as a kid; in fact, you loved them so much that when they re-form you want to go and see them as an adult. You think it will be good fun, to be a kid again, and share that with a roomful of adults reliving their happy childhood memories and all for a good cause. You see the show, and then, just before the end, one of them drops dead. You jump up on stage and end up saving the life of your childhood hero while the rest of the band sing 'Hot Potato'. If you asked any four-year-old what the best thing that could ever happen in your life would be, that is it.

15

FUTURE

I don't want to be one of those guys who think that everything was better in the olden days, but there was definitely one thing that was better in the olden days: the climate. It's become very apparent that we are no longer living through climate change, we are living a climate emergency.

Don't get me wrong. To me humanity is like the *Law & Order* TV franchise in that I know it will end at some stage, but I didn't think I would see it happen in my lifetime. But at the moment it seems like it is going to be a much closer race than I expected.

I might have been the only person who read the IPCC climate change report and thought, well, I guess the main thing I got out of that was, I don't have to quit smoking. If the fossil fuel companies are not going to quit, I certainly don't have to. In fact, I should start smoking more. Maybe I should roll up the pages of the report into a giant joint.

Things are accelerating faster than we imagined, and I have had to rethink what my personal future might look like. I was talking to my doctor about getting a hip operation for my OA and he was talking me through the risks and then he asked me what I was hoping to get from it. I think he was expecting me to say something like, 'To play some golf!' I don't think he expected me to say, 'Well, I'd like to be able to outrun the zombies when we are searching through the desert for clean drinking water!'

I used to have the same plan to combat climate change that most men my age seem to have: die before the major effects kick in. That is why I am not sure old people should get a say when it comes to climate change. A lot of old people don't worry too much about global warming; the warmer weather is better for their aching joints and they don't really care about the oceans rising. If we all need to live on boats they will be fine with that; it will just be like going on a really long cruise. Plus, they won't even have to worry about a *Titanic* situation with all the icebergs melted.

Old white men in particular have a lot of opinions about climate change for people who won't be around to face the consequences of it. Their attitude seems to be: 'Let's burn this coal! Let's Party Like It's 1799!'

And then when we got told the party needed to stop or the world would end, instead of leaving the party, we just turned down the music a little bit and kept partying. Although we did commission some reports that denied there was ever a party, and even if there was a party it certainly wasn't making any noise. But parties are pretty good for everyone. Who doesn't love a party? What are you, a party pooper? And then we kept partying, even harder than we had before, although we did commit to gradually winding down the party in about 30 years, as long as everyone else at the party also agreed to stop partying.

We are in real trouble and the only hope we have is that young people rise up more quickly than the oceans do. Young people are angry, and so they should be. We raised them telling them they had to clean up their own mess. And now it turns out they have to clean up our mess too. 'You know when we told you to clean your room? Now imagine your room is the entire planet!' They should put us in the naughty corner.

Maybe we should have a cut-off in what age you can be to make decisions that affect the future of the planet. Don't worry, you can still have opinions about things like cricket and biscuits. I am not sure our opinion should be weighted the same when we don't have the same stakes in what is being argued.

So often we hear the argument: 'Well, Wil, we can't leave the future generations with debt!' Yes, I get that, but I think they will deal with a few debts if it means they have a planet to live on. At the moment it feels like we are concentrating on paying off the mortgage when we don't realise that the house is completely wrecked from the nonstop party that has been happening inside. Let's be honest: the Earth is a rental, and we are not getting our bond back.

Even though I don't have kids of my own, I do believe older people owe it to the next generation to leave the place better than we found it. I always hear parents say things like, 'I would do anything for my kids. I would do absolutely anything for my kids.' Which is a lovely thing to say, but then when the kids reply, 'Well, what we would really like is an achievable and sustainable plan for the future survival of our planet,' suddenly the same parents say, 'Well, that seems quite hard. When I said I would do anything for you, what I was really thinking was a day at Bounce. You like trampolines, right? Maybe we can go to Wet'n'Wild—that will help prepare you for extreme weather conditions!'

16

MARCHING

Right now the kids are rightfully angry and demanding action. If none is taken, we'll have angry kids with no hope and that's destructive. You don't want to raise an entire generation without hope. No wonder they are angry. The question should be: why aren't we all just as angry?

Even worse when it comes to the next generation, their anger is often dismissed or minimised. Critics claim Greta Thunberg is being manipulated by her parents, and yet when David Attenborough says the same things as her, you don't hear the dismissals. 'Well, you know Sir Dave, always being manipulated by his parents. Yes, he is in his nineties, but he is constantly on the ouija board.'

The kids are so angry they took to the streets and people asked, 'Why are they protesting?' That shouldn't be the question. The question should be: 'Why aren't we all?'

Just like some suggest that immediately after a gun massacre is not the time to talk about reforming gun laws, some argue that natural disasters are not the time to protest about climate change. But the kids need to protest now. If they wait until they are in their thirties, they won't be able to protest because it will be too hot to go outside. The scariest thing of all is that this generation probably won't see the worst of it. There will be another generation after them who judge the way they live too. 'Oh, when you were young only ten percent of the country was on fire. Luxury!'

People will look for any excuse to invalidate kids' opinions. Some commentators got mad that kids swore at the marches. To which I say a hearty, 'Get fucked.' Of course they swore. But that is not the issue. They are more worried about rising seas than the c-word.

I actually went to the climate change march and a kid swore at me. And I was fine with it. I thought it was funny. He was twelve or thirteen. He spotted me in the crowd and said, 'Hey, OLD man . . . fuck you . . . this is all your fault!' I wasn't insulted by that—all I could think was, yeah, this kid gets it. He should be the leader. I admired him. I used to have that sort of passion back when I could have changed the world, but I got distracted.

Some kids skipped school and went on a climate change march, and some adults got mad about that. I never want to be an adult who gets mad at kids for caring. If I ever become that person you have my permission to slap me in the face with this book. I am excited that the kids give a shit; I am not going to be one of those adults who say, 'No, children, you shouldn't skip school to protest for the future of the place you live. You should stay in school and learn to follow orders without question.'

Some people asked, 'How is having a day off school going to prepare them for the real world?' Great question: how is it going to prepare them for life in the real world? The real world where we have a day off for the footy Grand Final, and the Queen's birthday which wasn't even on her actual birthday? And that was before Covid hit and they suddenly had a lot more days off school. In fact, it would have prepared them pretty well.

Turns out you can miss a day or two of school. What are you going to learn in school that day that is more important than the future of the planet? Oh no, we will have a generation of kids who don't understand the Dewey Decimal System! Guess what, I was at school when they taught that and I still don't understand it. Is it still even a thing? I think if it's important enough, they will go back over it again the next day. I don't think there is anyone saying, 'I don't know how to read! They taught us everything about reading on the day I was off at a protest and they refused to go back over it.'

Kids can miss a day of school. I don't think we are suddenly going to have an entire generation who are saying, 'I missed a day of geography and now I can't tell direction and the only job I will be able to get is as a taxi driver'; or 'You think that's bad, I missed a day of maths and now I can't add up properly and the only job I can get is as an accountant for a billionaire'; or 'That's tough, but I missed a day of science and now I know nothing about science and the only job I can get is homeopath or Liberal Party environment minister.'

Some people said, 'Not everyone at the march believed in the cause. Some of the kids just wanted a day off school.' Well, duh! What? Shut up! Some kids wanted the day off school? Well then, that delegitimises the entire argument, doesn't it?

At least when they wagged school they were doing it for something important. When I wagged school I did it to fill in for my mum's netball team. It was a daytime league, so if they were one short I would get the day off and go and play netball with a bunch of mums. And I would dominate. They really were my most glorious sporting years, but I couldn't boast about it. It's not cool to come back to school and get in another kid's face and say, 'I kicked your mum's arse at netball today!'

The position I used to play was generally Wing Attack. I think it was because the regular Wing Attack was the person who was most often unavailable, but I liked to think it was because I could wear my initials on my back. It would have been better if it were my dad's netball team. He is Graeme Anderson, so he could have played Goal Attack. (My mum's name is Chris, but there is no CA on the netball court, although Coal Attack is I guess what the climate protestors are doing.) I used to like playing netball. It's a great game, plus it's one of the few places where a white man can raise his arm up straight in public and not be accused of trying to start a rally. But just to be safe, I would only guard someone to three-quarters elevation.

The game only went for an hour, but if I played well I would get the whole day off and Mum and I would go to Muffin Break together where I would eat the top off the muffins and she would eat the bottom. My favourite thing about the game of netball is that you don't call for the ball. You say, 'Here if you need!' That's a life philosophy if you ever need one: sometimes you don't need to insert yourself in someone else's business, but you might say, 'Here if you need.'

The reason I went to the kids' climate march was that netball ethos. I wanted to say to the next generation, 'I support you in this fight, and I am here if you need.' Some commentators argued that the kids had been brainwashed by the teachers. Okay, for starters, you're lucky if brainwashing is the only way you get interfered with at school. Plus, we got brainwashed when we were at school. Not by the teachers, but by what they were teaching. We got taught that Captain Cook discovered Australia, which is like me walking into a cafe, sitting at someone else's table and saying I discovered their avocado smash. The thing they don't warn you about education is that it's not just the years you spend learning stuff, it's all the years you have to spend to unlearn some shit too. But here's how I know teachers can't brainwash. If teachers were able to brainwash, I would be able to speak French. Instead I did six years of it at high school and this is the French I know: croissant. Pepé Le Pew. Henri Leconte. I can't even French kiss. I have tried several times to communicate with a French bulldog and I still can't understand a word they say.

At the time, the PM, Scott Morrison, said that we don't want our schools turned into parliaments. On that point we agree. I would hope schools have much higher standards than parliaments. We don't want our kids behaving that badly. In parliaments they lie, they cheat and they steal. They look after the powerful instead of the weak. And they only have a handful of sitting days a year. How is that going to prepare them for life in the real world?

17

OZONE

Kids being passionate about the environment isn't a new thing. When I was in Year 11, back when I last had potential, I was so filled with potential that I decided to write a play. Every year we would have a drama competition where each of the four school houses would stage a 30-minute play in front of the entire school. Because 30-minute plays are hard to find, it would usually end up being some one-act play where a bunch of children pretended to be adults talking about issues that none of the people in the play really understood, and certainly no-one in the audience enjoyed. The other downside was that most of these one-act plays only had a small cast so only a few kids would get to perform.

I thought there had to be a better way of doing things, and our house had traditionally been terrible at this competition, so I made a pitch to our leaders that they should let me take over the whole thing. They were happy to let me do it: one thing off their plate. My ambitious plan was to let anyone who wanted to be in the play audition, and then I would write a role that was commensurate to their talent or confidence level. If they wanted to be in the show but could only deliver one line, then I would write them a part that consisted of only one line. But most importantly, they would get to be in the show. I didn't have a show, but I had a theme about a major issue of the time, and a title: *Murder on The Ozone Express*.

I held the auditions and ended up with a cast in the mid-twenties, more than three times larger than the next biggest. Once the auditions were done I started writing the show, although 'writing' is a very generous term. More taking my favourite bits from various comedies and sketches that I had seen and then ordering them into some kind of coherent narrative. I might not have always directly ripped off some classic comedy bits, but they would have had a lot of shared family tree on ancestry.com. Or, to put it another way, if I'd had to release the play as an album there would have been more samples to clear than The Avalanches' first album.

The original subjects of the jokes were replaced by teachers or other people who worked at the school, which I knew would be the ultimate crowd pleasers in a hall filled with bored students. This was a good plan. The only flaw was that the script had to be submitted to the school for approval to make sure there wasn't any inappropriate material. My script was mostly inappropriate material. About five percent plot, five percent theme and 90 percent inappropriate material. It turned out the teachers agreed with my assessment, and my script came back with so many jokes edited out, it looked like a redacted document you'd find on WikiLeaks.

My play had shrunk from 30 minutes to ten at best. Now I had a dilemma. I knew that all the jokes the teachers didn't like were the exact same ones that the 400 kids in the assembly hall were going to love. Even then, I wasn't trying to please the teachers, I wanted to play the audience. So what should I do? The teachers told me the only option was to substantially rewrite the play, but another option occurred to me. I could just not tell the cast about the changes. In my head, I was so certain we would win, everyone would love it, and I could deal with the fallout once we won. They say it is better to apologise than ask for permission. Technically I had been denied permission but I thought fuck it, and did it anyway.

Luckily my instincts were right and *Murder on The Ozone Express* won the assembly room audience and the house drama competition as well. Of course I did get in trouble for directly disobeying the teachers' instructions, but hearing that whole hall roaring with laughter had been worth it. Also, I think it is important to note, I did learn my lesson. The next year I got the cast to rehearse all the jokes in the sequel, *Gunfight at the Ozone Corral*, but just gave the teachers a script without the jokes in it to approve. Problem solved. I don't know what happened to those plays or if the scripts still exist, but I do know that if I had written a poem denying climate change it would still be quoted by politicians to this day.

At this point younger readers, if there are any, might be asking: what is the obsession with ozone? And also, what is ozone? Is it like Timezone? Or is it that show on Netflix about that money-laundering family? (Not really a spoiler for the TV show *Ozark*, but a funny side note is that early on it is revealed that the money laundering leads to their one day having enough money to escape to their dream destination, which is, I kid you not, Mullumbimby, New South Wales. 'One day, kids, we will have enough money for all the Apple Cider Vinegar you have ever wanted. Rivers of gold.')

Well, kids, gather around and I will tell you the Tale of Ozone. Before you were all marching about climate change, the biggest environmental concern of my generation was the hole in the ozone layer. In fact, I had a climate-change denier recently telling me that global warming was just the latest manufactured panic and asked, 'I mean, what happened to the hole in the ozone layer?'

I am actually glad you asked, my friend. There was a hole in the ozone layer and the governments of the world got together and decided it would be better for everyone if there wasn't. So in order to do something about that they came up with something called the Montreal Protocol, which sounds like a Matt Damon movie—*Matt Damon is Johnny Montreal*—but is even cooler than that sounds. You see, they had worked out that there were these things called CFCs.

Did somebody say CFCs? Yes, I did just then. CFC stands for chlorofluorocarbons or Collingwood Football Club, I can't remember which. Either way, scientists had discovered that CFCs were being real F's and C's and had been damaging the ozone layer for over half a century, so the governments of the world did something pretty controversial and believed the scientists and banned the CFCs.

When we stopped using CFCs the ozone layer started to recover and is still continuing to repair itself, and this is all because world leaders worked together and believed science, although the latest IPCC report revealed that my school plays helped a lot as well.

18

KIDS

I've never understood the impulse to judge the younger generation. For starters, if the kids are no good then that is not their fault. That is *your* fault. They are *your* kids. But I think we have to give the next generation all the support we can, especially as they have a big job in front of them: cleaning up our mistakes.

There's never been an easy time to be a human. In some ways we live in the greatest of times, with technology that I couldn't even imagine when I was a kid. But we have been through some hard times, and if we are paying attention we know there are probably even harder times ahead. I am sorry if that is a glass-half-empty approach, but when the oceans are half full with plastic, it's hard to be otherwise.

I think it is amazing, with all we know about climate change, that people still have kids. When someone asks if I have any 'protection', I whip out a copy of the IPCC report.

How do people still have kids? I mean seriously, how do they do it? Can you show me some pictures? I am not really sure myself; I missed that day of sex education because I was at a protest.

When I see pregnant people, I need to resist my impulse to go up to them and ask, 'What's your secret? Do you not read newspapers? How do you think this is a good idea? I am not judging, I want to feel like that too. Have you heard of climate change? Instead of playing them music in the womb, are you going to play them episodes of Bear Grylls? Are you going to give them a water birth to get them used to the conditions they will face?'

I don't know how I would handle that, the knowledge that your kid is going to grow up in a world where *Mad Max: Fury Road* has gone from an awesome movie to a terrifying documentary. If my child did not come out, cut its own umbilical cord and eat the placenta, then I would feel like I had failed at being a parent already.

I don't have any kids, which I think should be taken into consideration for my Order of Australia. (Side note: My grandfather and father have both received the Order of Australia. I also have an OA: osteoarthritis.) At the very least I think I should get credit for not having kids if I ever forget my Keep Cup at the cafe. Yes, I forgot my cup, but you've got four kids, mate . . . Why don't you keep it in your pants?

Just because I don't have children of my own doesn't mean I don't care about other people's. That's a misconception;

for starters, I have three nieces with red hair and I would like them to grow up in a world where they don't explode when they go outside.

When the Covid pandemic hit, I didn't feel like much of my life was prepared for it, but the one thing that did make me feel like a Doomsday prepper was the decision not to have children. I could barely handle my own life during that time, so I don't know how people managed it with their kids.

About six months after moving, I finally had guests visit for the first time. It's amazing how you can live in a house for so long but it doesn't feel like a home until other people come to visit. The new rules allowed two couples each with kids of similar ages to come over for the day. I gave them the instructions for how to find the place and warned them that the road from Mullumbimby was winding, so pay attention (I didn't want to tell them just how dangerous it was; I wanted them to come).

I loved that they were bringing their kids. Just because I don't have any doesn't mean I don't like them. I like lions too, but I don't want to get one for the house. I love my friends' kids; in fact, sometimes I think I love them more than their parents do, because I get to see them at their best. When I get to see them, their parents are showing them off. They've cleaned them up. The kids are in a good mood because their parents are letting them do things they normally wouldn't to keep them happy. I get all the fun and none of the consequences.

Plus, I get to be the Cool Uncle, and because I tend to live like a kid who gets to buy his own stuff, my house is always filled with things that kids love, like lollies and chocolates and chips and cake and ice-cream. It turns out that kids at a party and stoners tend to have a lot of food choices in common.

Because the parents all want to talk to other adults, the kids not only get to have snack food they wouldn't normally get, but also to sit on the couch and play video games. I have a PlayStation that I never use myself but which is really good for these situations. The only downside is that I don't have any games for kids, so they have to play the games that I have. Which the kids love, and the parents make an exemption in return for some peace and quiet.

And that is how four primary school boys ended up sitting on the couch in my house eating sugar and playing *Mortal Kombat* and *Grand Theft Auto*, and why I got all the cool points. Of course they didn't tell me that, but they did apparently go to school and tell all their mates. Unfortunately, they also told someone they couldn't trust, because apparently one day there was a policeman at their school doing a presentation and one of the other kids told him the four boys had played *Grand Theft Auto* and asked if the policeman was going to arrest them. I was proud when I heard that story, but I did tell them to remind that other kid that snitches get stitches.

19

BEES

Because I don't have my own children, I only have one way to talk to kids. Basically I talk to them as if they are adults. I don't mean I use adult concepts or language, I mean I literally talk to them as if I have mistaken them for an adult and can't work out why they are pretending to be a kid.

Occasionally I will meet a kid who is not there for my bullshit, but in general it works quite well. I ask, 'How was work today?' And when they reply, 'I don't have a job,' I will continue the conversation by saying something like, 'Oh, I am sorry, I didn't know you'd lost your job. Did you get fired?' And then take it from there. Although it can go wrong: one day I asked a kid how their marriage was going and they replied that they weren't married, they were only six. I said, 'Not married at six, hmmm, that's weird,' and they said, 'You're really old and you're not married—*you're* weird!' Touché.

My friend and I were sitting by the pool while his kids swam. Suddenly a swarm of bees flew in and landed on the edge of the pool. This was not an uncommon thing. The bees would come to the pool, which they used for water and temperature regulation. I had been trying to work out ways to deal with it without harming the bees. Bees are endangered and vital for humanity, so I definitely didn't want to kill them, but I wanted to keep them away from the pool. With that in mind I hadn't been using any chemicals to try to keep them away. Instead I had been using peppermint oil. Peppermint oil is better for the bees because it doesn't work. But on the upside, you have a pool that smells like toothpaste.

I wanted to reassure the kids, so I told them not to worry about the bees. The area the bees liked to gather in was well away from where the kids were, and in general they don't attack unless provoked. That seemed to reassure them, and they kept playing. After a while, attracted by the splashing, the bees did start to fly around a little and one of my friends' kids grew a bit more nervous.

I told him that I knew the bees and they wouldn't attack. But then I went too far. Spotting that my friends' kid was wearing yellow and black swimmers, I added, 'Those bees are all friendly, there is only one who is mean and deadly— I can't remember which one he is but the good news is he only attacks if he sees something that looks like a bigger bee and needs to defend himself. So as long as no-one here is wearing the same colours as a bee, then we should be safe!'

Not the funniest joke of all time, but good Cool Uncle gear, I thought.

I don't know if you have ever made a friends' child cry, but it turns out it can happen really suddenly and it is not a nice feeling. Apparently I am not as bad an actor as I thought, because he had bought the whole story and was now in fear for his life from the attack of this killer bee. How was he? He was not fine. He was sobbing and trying to rip his swimmers off when his dad stepped in, hugged him and in that moment delivered me one of the greatest burns of all time when he said to his weeping child, 'You know how I told you in the car that Wil was a comedian? Well, that was just one of his jokes.'

I don't have kids, but I do have pets. Now, before anyone with kids reading this complains that having pets is not the same thing as having kids, I agree. They are not the same. For example, if my kid was ten and still taking a dump in the street I am not sure I would be walking behind them and picking it up. I certainly wouldn't be patting them on the head and telling them they were a good boy.

Humans tend to say we have pets because we love animals, but if we are being completely honest it's because we love *some* animals. For them to have a nice life we occasionally feed them meat, which means I guess those dead animals we are feeding them didn't really feel the love. Personally I like to think the dried kangaroo tendon my dog is currently chewing on was donated by a very generous kangaroo that had filled out their donor card. 'I won't be needing this where I am going. Make sure it goes to a good home.'

I guess you could make the argument that people who really love animals are those who choose not to have pets: 'I decided that instead of loving a kitten up close, I would love 100 cows from afar!'

I've not eaten meat in more than 20 years, but I will feed my pets meat regularly. One day when our cat was old and not feeling well, I even ordered him sushi on Uber Eats. That pretty much goes against everything I believe in, but I did it because he needed to eat and wouldn't get excited about any of his regular food. It turns out that he was excited about sushi. I know this is indulgent, but if you have a cat, once in their life get them sushi. It will be the best day of their life. Of course they love it—it's basically all the same ingredients they have in their normal diet, but higher quality. They go bananas. It's the best thing they have ever tasted. It's like the first time you try food when stoned. In fact, don't order in. I would suggest getting them dressed up and taking them to the restaurant. It will be the best night of your life, and theirs. Cats love sashimi, but they hate wasabi. Yeah, I found that out the hard way. In his defence, the cat thought it was avocado. And I guess I should point out that they find the chopsticks a little tricky at first, but it's culturally respectful, so persist. If you need to, sticky-tape the sticks to their paws, then pour some milk into the little soy bowl. They will be so happy.

20

WOOD

The new house came with an old iron wood stove for heating, and even better news, the previous owners reported they had recently had a couple of trees chopped for wood and there was a wood pile that would last at least a couple of winters.

They explained that the wood pile was under a tarpaulin on the furthest edge of the property, down a path and through some trees, but it would be easy to spot. They asked if I wanted them to show me where it was, but I felt like that was a little patronising. I think I can spot a huge pile of wood. It was hardly a needle in a haystack. In fact, it was more a wood-stack in a paddock so I should be fine. I am an observational comedian; I will use my professional powers of observation. I don't have any other use for them at the moment. Plus, I decided it could be a project. Find the wood pile and then light a fire for the house. That would be what I would do the next day.

The next morning I set out to find my wood pile. I walked down the path and through the trees, but didn't see it. So I kept walking. And walking. My hips were starting to hurt and I was starting to regret my decision to turn down the offer to show me where it was. I couldn't go back without wood now; I had gone too far. I walked a little further and spotted a blue tarp another couple of hundred metres away. Okay, that must be it. It was further away than I had expected, but on the upside it turned out I had mistakenly bought a property that was bigger than I thought. I probably mixed up hectares with acres. For some reason I have never been able to retain which is which. I looked it up to write this sentence and have already forgotten.

As I walked back to the house, all I could think about was why you would have the wood pile so far from the house. Was it some kind of country wisdom that I didn't understand? You keep the wood as far away as you can from its eventual fate. It's just basic courtesy, plus you don't want the other trees to find out and start plotting against you. The walk was inconvenient, so I made a plan. I had nothing to do with my days, so it would be good to have a project. I decided to move the wood pile closer to the house. The next day I set out with my wheelbarrow and started moving the wood. By the end of the week I had moved over half of the pile and restacked it into an impressive pile closer to home. I was very proud of my work.

Maybe I would be okay at this country life after all. When everything was falling apart, it felt good that there was one thing I could control. And every night I would celebrate by lighting the wood stove and heating the house. Seeing the pets sleeping in the warmth of my day's work warmed me.

So one morning, when I set out with my wheelbarrow, it was quite a shock when I spotted someone taking wood out of my original wood pile and loading it into the back of his ute. I thought, 'Shit . . . that is not my wood pile.'

I immediately knew what had happened. It all made sense. I knew my property wasn't *that* big. I knew I was walking too far. Clearly I had been setting out every day, walking past my wood pile that I, as an observational comedian, had not observed, over to a neighbour's property before grabbing wood out of their wood pile. And not a small amount of wood, not a 'Please, sir, just enough for us to survive the winter' amount. I had been literally loading wheelbarrows full of his wood and moving it closer to my house. I hadn't even destroyed the evidence. I could have at least burned it, but it was stacked over by my house. There's no real way to deny that. 'Yeah, mate, I don't know what happened. I just woke up one morning and it was there. Climate change, I guess?'

I also couldn't deny it was me, as I was holding a wheelbarrow. Great. Another show about being arrested, coming soon: *Wil Barrow.*

This was a disaster. When you move to a new neighbourhood, you want to prove to them that you are a good neighbour.

Everybody needs good neighbours; it's basically our unofficial national anthem, and one of the easiest ways you can do that is by not stealing their stuff. It should be the easiest one to lock in, but I had stumbled at the first hurdle. Or more accurately, I had grabbed the first hurdle and moved it closer to my house. 'Have you met the Andersons? Nice people, but all I would say is keep your eye on your wood, if you know what I mean?'

'I am not sure I do know what you mean, but I will be sure to hide my cricket bats and cuckoo clocks when he's around.'

I was in the wrong. There was no way I could blame this on anyone else. I only had one option. I just had to apologise and hope he saw the funny side. I mean, once you got over the initial shock, it was pretty funny. Surely it would be clear that I'd made a mistake, I mean otherwise it would be the most brazen crime in history. Just move the wood closer to the house and then gaslight him into thinking it had always been there. That is a way to assert your dominance in a new neighbourhood. Surely if I just explained, he would find it funny. And then I could just wheel all the wood back, and the stuff I'd burned I would replace from my wood pile. (When I found it.)

So I walked up to this man I had been stealing from for a week and my mind was racing. Before I could even start my apology, he said, 'Oh, g'day, mate. How are you?'

How . . . am . . . I? Here's how I am: I am not fine. I knew I couldn't tell him how I really was, so instead I said, 'So, this is a really weird situation. I am so sorry!'

He looked at me, paused for a little longer than was comfortable for me, and I started to worry about what was coming next. Was he going to yell at me? Punch me? Shame me?

He said, 'I know, right, but shit happens, honest mistake, no worries!'

No worries! Never have two words meant more to me. It came as such a relief, because to be honest with you I had lots of worries. Hundreds of worries. I didn't even know that having zero worries was one of the available options. I would have considered walking away from the whole thing with fewer than ten worries a victory. I was not a warrior, I was a worrier. But 'No worries' was the attitude I had moved to this part of the world for, and I thought I should learn from this guy and his attitude. He's cool. He's glass-half-full. This is who I need to be.

Above all else I was grateful. Grateful that he didn't make me feel bad about my mistake. I appreciated it. I appreciated it so much that I completely started overcompensating and helping him load wood into his ute. I even took the wheelbarrow back to the pile closer to the house, wheeled it back and loaded it in the ute too. When the tray was finally full he turned to me, shook my hand and said, 'Nice to meet you, mate. Thanks for being so cool about this. I didn't know that anyone was living here and I just thought I could take this wood.'

Shit. Shit, shit, shit, shit, shit. It *was* my wood pile. No wonder he had been so cool about me stealing from him:

I *hadn't* been stealing from him. *He* had been stealing from *me*. No wonder he had no worries. He had been busted stealing and instead of someone yelling at him, punching him or shaming him, they had instead started loading more wood in the back of his ute. Not only that, they had gone to another wood pile and got more wood from that as well. 'Please, sir, take my wood. I was throwing it out anyway. It was actually a deconstructed tree that I got at Ikea and I have lost a couple of parts so it was basically hard rubbish.'

There was part of me that wanted to be angry, but it was way too late now. I was just embarrassed. He might have been a thief, but I didn't want him to think I was an idiot. As he drove off with a load of my wood, all I could think was I hoped one night he was in prison—not for this crime—where he was watching *Gruen* and he turned to his cellmate. 'You know, one night I stole some wood from him. And he was really cool about it. Actually loaded some wood in my ute. Nice guy. Good neighbour.'

21

MASKS

My general setting is not wanting to make a fuss. As long as your beliefs don't hurt anyone else, then I respect them. But I have also always subscribed to the idea that when you live in a community, the right to swing your fist stops at the other person's face. Living in my new home during the pandemic challenged those instincts on many levels. How do you live in a place where people think completely the opposite from you? The most obvious example was masks, and the major difference of opinion was that I wore one and no-one else did.

At the start of the pandemic, friends in Melbourne asked me, 'Are people wearing masks in the shops in Mullumbimby?' I would laugh. People didn't wear masks in the shops in Mullumbimby. People didn't wear shoes in the shops in Mullumbimby. People didn't wear *shirts* in the shops in Mullumbimby, and this is just the staff I am talking about. You know that expression,

'No shoes, no shirt, no service'? They have the opposite: 'Shoes, shirt? What are you, an undercover cop? Get out of here, narc!'

Of course, most people do wear shoes at the shops, but definitely not all, and I think if I am being honest I was more disturbed by the not wearing shoes than I was by the not wearing masks. For me the only reason you should be in a shop with no shoes is if someone just stole them and you have come in to buy some new ones. I remember at the start of it all when there was a shortage of masks, a viral video hack showed how you could make one out of a sock. I remember thinking, 'That doesn't help: they are not wearing socks here either!'

No-one wore a mask in town, but I shouldn't judge because they all had a medical mask exemption. I am sure there are people who had a legitimate medical reason not to wear a mask, and it was just coincidence that 95 percent of them happened to live in Mullumbimby. Again, I shouldn't judge. Maybe they all had the same fake ailment. Fake ailments can be highly contagious.

I did hear one person explain that the reason they couldn't wear the mask was they couldn't breathe through it. That their lungs were just not strong enough to be able to breathe through all that heavy fabric. That seemed like a very fair excuse apart from the fact I had recently seen them sucking back a bucket bong. The old lungs seemed to be working pretty well that night as they sucked smoke through three foot of garden hose. Somehow I think if we had put a mask between them and the bong, they still would have managed to get the marijuana inside their lungs.

Some people didn't even bother with a medical excuse; they just complained that the masks weren't comfortable. Yeah, no shit. I get that. I don't wear them because they are comfortable, but they are more comfortable than lying in a hospital bed with a machine breathing for me, so I went with that. In fact, I often wore a second mask to keep my first mask on because the masks don't stay on my face. You see, I have weird ears that join to my head at the bottom; I don't have traditional lobes. It really hadn't been a problem in my life until masks came along and I realised I didn't have anything to hook them on to. So instead what tends to happen is the mask just pulls my ears out so my head looks like a Mintie.

Of course I knew, and most people probably knew, that the majority of those who claimed to have a medical exemption didn't have one, but we all pretended that they did and then got on with things. But the ones that really committed to the lie made me laugh. The ones who would be adamant: 'No, I really did get an exemption. My doctor said I can't wear the mask.' Well, now, I know it is definitely not true because you don't go to the actual doctor. You don't believe in traditional medicine. If you want health advice you go to a TV chef, and a TV chef can write you a recipe but they can't write you a medical exemption. Oh, your doctor wrote you an exemption, did they? And what is the name of your doctor? 'Yes, he's a very reputable doctor, his name is Dr Seuss. You might have heard of him. He has written heaps of books. He wrote this: "She does not need the mask you see, she trusts her natural immunity. To her the mask is an affront, because she is a selfish . . ." I can't read his handwriting, I can't make out that last word.'

The truth was you didn't need a mask exemption most places, because no-one was asking you to wear one. Of course they couldn't legally say that you didn't need to wear a mask, so instead they used a code: 'We don't discriminate'. That is one of those things that sounds good. Discrimination is a bad thing and they don't discriminate. Which is also something they had in common with Covid.

But the twist was that in the end there were some who did discriminate. Against vaccinated people. This is true. Recently vaccinated people were banned from some businesses because they thought you could shed the vaccine and people could get accidentally vaccinated. When I heard about this, I didn't tell anyone I was getting my second vaccine. I booked in first thing in the morning so no-one would spot me, and so I could have the rest of the day to shed. That day I shed like no-one has ever shed before. I had a long breakfast and shed in the cafe, I went shopping and shed in the supermarket, I shed all over the fresh fruit and vegetables. If there was any truth to what they were saying (and to be clear, there is not), then I was a hero. I was potentially saving lives and surely that's a good loophole for the anti-vaxxers: you didn't get the vaccine, you just caught the vaccine from someone else. So that day

I shed. I shed in the health food store, and in the incense shop I shed all over the crystals. Forget Mr Ed, I was Mr Shed. I was The Duke Of Shedinburgh. I went into the linen store and shed on the bedding, I went into the hardware shop and shed in an actual shed. That one probably didn't help, but it felt appropriate.

There were those of us who wore masks, those who didn't, and I can understand the reasoning of both, even if I don't agree with it all. But there is a third group of people who absolutely fascinate me: the people who wear a mask, but decide to wear it around their chin.

I want to get inside the head of these people. What is going on? Did you get a mask exemption but only for part of your face? I don't understand the idea of going to all the effort of sourcing the mask, buying the mask, putting the mask on your face, but not putting it anywhere on your face where it will actually prevent Covid. That's all the inconvenience with none of the benefit.

But there they were with their masks proudly hung around their chin. 'Well, if that doesn't scare off Covid then nothing will.' Yes, something will: moving that mask up over your nose and mouth. The mask doesn't scare Covid off; it is not a warning flag or Aerogard. The only way it really works is if you put it over your Covid holes to stop the Covid getting in. Actually, while I think about it, did you cover that manhole with the tarpaulin so the children playing nearby won't fall in? Or did you just put the tarp near the manhole and assume it would warn the kids? Is that how you live your whole life? 'Yes, I bought a bulletproof jacket but I only wear it slung over my shoulder, that's just how I roll. I will wear a condom but only over my testicles.'

I wore a mask, I still wear a mask and I can't see a time when I will take it off. The main reason I wear a mask is protection. Not to keep the Covid out, but to keep my opinions in. I wear a mask to protect the community from what I am really thinking. That has been my biggest lesson in the past couple of years, how often I have had to bite my tongue. Masks have helped.

One morning I was in line for takeaway at a restaurant. I was social distancing and I was wearing a mask. There were two mothers in front of me who were facing forward, their backs to me, weren't wearing masks and were talking at such a volume that I don't feel bad repeating this story. One mother turned to the other and said, 'I don't trust the Covid tests, I would never get one. In fact, I don't even let my kids do the temperature test.'

The other woman turned to her and asked, 'Why?' And I have to admit I was glad she asked. I shared her curiosity. In the Before Times I would have leaned in to hear more, but I maintained my social distance and just tried to listen harder.

The original mum replied, 'Well, you know my five-year-old? The other morning we were at a restaurant and he got the temperature test and since then he has been really forgetful. I think they might have wiped his memory.'

115

The shocked other mum asked, 'Really?'

And I didn't hear the reply to that because I was too busy grabbing extra masks from my pocket and jamming them over the top of the mask I was already wearing to stop the words coming out. Because all I wanted to do was scream, 'No! Not really! That is not real! How can we agree on how to fight this virus when we can't even agree on basic truth? For starters, that technology does not exist, you are thinking about the movie franchise *Men in Black*. Secondly, if that technology did exist and the government had access to it, do you really think administering it at random restaurants is how they would use it? That seems highly impractical. "Excuse me, sir, what would you like to order?" "I don't know. What restaurant is this? I can't remember why I came here. Actually, what's a restaurant and who am I?" But let's give you the benefit of the doubt, and entertain the idea that this technology does exist, and the government has access to it, and they are administering it at random restaurants to shut people up who know too much. If that is true, what the fuck did your kid stumble onto that needed to be covered up? Did he work out who Q is? Is it Bluey? Is it Quey? Want to know why your kid is forgetful? He is five. I mean, what did he forget exactly? Did he miss an important meeting? Did he forget the last three digits of his crypto code? If you are looking for reasons your kid might be forgetting stuff, I would start with the second-hand bong smoke in the living room!'

That's what I wanted to say, but I didn't, and that's why I wear a mask. It saves lives, mostly mine.

I think the pandemic has been toughest on the young. They have had to sacrifice so much for the rest of us and miss so many important life events they will never get back. I hope we remember that. I admire the young, but I am also very aware that I am not one of them anymore.

I am not young, I am middle-aged. I know that I am because on the morning of my 45th birthday, I received a message from a dear friend. I was doing breakfast radio, so my alarm would sound at four thirty each morning, but when I got up and checked my phone I already had one message. It said, 'Welcome to middle age!'

What. The. Fuck? It was way too early for me to process this information. I couldn't be middle-aged, I am still young and cool. I used to be on Triple J. Next you'll be telling me I am old enough to have a doctor who is ten years younger than me. Sure, I knew I was turning 45, that was not a surprise to me, but the idea that that qualified me as middle-aged certainly was. He couldn't be right.

I couldn't get on with my day before I knew for sure. I had to check the dictionary, and yes, I didn't google it, I checked an actual dictionary—which I guess in retrospect was probably a clue—and looked up the definition of middle-aged. My friend was right. It turns out the dictionary definition of middle-aged is: 'Whatever age you are when you look up the dictionary definition of middle-aged.'

According to the dictionary, the definition of middle-aged is 45 to 65. That makes me think that definition was invented by someone who was already in their sixties. Calling 65 middle-aged seems a tad optimistic. You are only going to be middle-aged at 65 if you are planning on being the oldest person in the world. Do you think the oldest person in the world ever looks back and thinks, 'That explains my behaviour when I was 65: I was having a midlife crisis. No wonder I quit my job, got a new car and traded in my wife for a younger model. And when I say I quit my job, I actually retired, my new car was an electric mobility scooter, and I didn't really trade in my old wife—she died of natural causes. And my new wife was actually 55, but what a firecracker.'

I'm a middle-aged middle-class white mostly cisgender Australian man. So you get it, it's been tough. The struggle is real. Where's my march? Am I right? Actually there are a bunch of marches that are mostly made up of men who look like me, but they never seem to be for fun causes.

As a white man I would like to take this moment to say on behalf of my people, 'Oops. Sorry.'

I find it weird when white men complain about the war on white men. Come on, guys, we've had a good run. It's been good to be a straight white middle-aged man pretty much from the beginning of time . . . up until about six months ago. And it's still fine, but things have got a little wobbly.

Of course not everyone is happy about jokes about straight white middle-aged men. And I know that because I read my own emails. One guy messaged me and said making fun of straight white men was punching down. No, it's punching myself. Stop hitting me, me, stop hitting me.

I get that compared to most I am privileged. And I also get that a lot of people don't share that same privilege, and that makes life, and the pandemic, even harder to deal with. I have no problem acknowledging the privileges I have in society, and I always find it weird when people do. I think sometimes when we say to white men that they are privileged, what they hear is that they didn't work hard for what they have. That's not what it means. You can work hard and still be privileged. And you can still get screwed over by life despite your privilege.

Personally I don't think it takes anything away from what I have done in life to acknowledge my privileges. I am from three generations of farmers who lived in a place of 250 people. The first person I met who worked in show business was me. I worked hard for what I have, but that doesn't mean that a woman in the exact same circumstances would not have had to work harder. Or a person of colour, a refugee, a person with a disability; the list goes on.

Being a white man, a white Australian man, is like being at the Olympics and you have trained as hard as you can for your event, and on the day you run as fast as you can. But what you don't realise is that there is a slight tail breeze in your lane. And the woman in the lane to your left doesn't have that breeze, and they have made her run in high heels for some reason, and the person of colour running next to her is in a lane that is uphill and they've been made to start 10 metres back, and the refugee has to start 20 metres back and in a boat and there is no water, and the person in a wheelchair has hurdles in their lane, which just seems cruel. And then you don't even win because there is a rich fucker in the lane to your right who is not even running, he is riding a golden unicorn.

White men have been like the Harlem Globetrotters—if the Harlem Globetrotters didn't realise the game was rigged for them to win. We have just been walking around like we are the best basketball players in the world. We have had Globetrotter privilege. We have been breaking the rules, and literally standing on the shoulders of others to dunk on them. We have been pulling down our opponents' pants and everyone laughs and says: Globetrotters will be Globetrotters.

I've had to check my privilege many times in conversations with people I like but don't agree with. Luckily, as a professional entertainer I don't really like to talk unless I am getting paid for it, so I have got very good at listening. I like listening to what people think about the world, and trying to understand why they think like that, and I do believe you can listen to someone without having to agree with them.

I don't have all the answers, so instead I have listened. A lot. And I have learned a lot about myself. There is one expression in particular I have heard over and over: 'You know what your problem is, Wil?'

I love when someone asks me this, because I feel like I am playing a game. I do know what my problem is. In fact,

I know what *all* my problems are, and I have a lot of them. Move over, Jay-Z, 99 problems is just my first page. I know what my problems are, but I am always keen for a stranger to have a guess.

Let's see if you can nail one.

'You know what your problem is, Wil? You don't do your own research. I didn't take the vaccine because I did my own research. What do you think about that?'

Well, I think . . . that you are bad at research. I think you should stop doing research and do something that you are actually good at. There is no shame in not being good at research; it's a skill people take years to develop. I am sure you are good at something else. I think you should go and work in an orchard, because you are great at cherrypicking. Or maybe you should become a junior footy coach; you are great at moving the goalposts.

But they are right. I don't do my own research. Sure, I google lots of things that don't matter, but I don't do research on things like vaccines because I am not qualified to do research. I don't know what a null hypothesis or p-value is. To me they sound like a New Zealand hip-hop outfit. I am not sure why, it just feels right. 'Kia ora, bro, I'm P-Value and he is Null Hypothesis . . . How many dudes you know can research like this? Not many, if any . . .'

I did have one person ask me a question where the answer seemed so simple I thought it must be a trap. They said, 'If you won't do your own research, what do you do, just trust experts?'

I couldn't think of any other answer than yes. So I said, 'Yes?' *Baaa.*

His eyes lit up like he had me just where he wanted me. 'But experts don't always get it right!'

I know that experts don't always get it right. I just think that experts get it right more often than dickheads. That is the only assumption I make on a daily basis, in this situation when deciding who I should trust out of an expert or a dickhead. (Side note: If you are a dickhead reading this, know that it's okay for me to make this joke because I am also a dickhead. In fact, most of the time when I have decided expert over dickhead, the dickhead in question is me.)

I trust experts because in general I think they know more about stuff than me, a non-expert. It seems quite a decent system to run the world, really. I don't have time to learn how to do everything myself. That would be a terrible system. 'Hey, Wil, your comedy festival show was pretty crap this year. Why was that?' Sadly, I spent all the time I should have been writing the show learning how to build a car so I could drive to the gig.

I know that experts can get things wrong. That's why the best science isn't just one person's opinion, it's a consensus of opinion that has been peer-reviewed and tested. That's why your doctor will tell you to get a second opinion, but they mean get a second opinion from another doctor. They don't mean, 'Well, that's my take, but also I would suggest Doctor Google, seeing what your Facebook friends think, and don't you have an uncle or someone you can run it by?'

I know that experts don't always get it right. I am a stand-up comedian. If people just trusted experts, they would laugh at all my jokes whether they got them or not. 'Ha ha . . . I didn't really get that one, but he has been doing this for 25 years and I only come once or twice a year so I guess I should trust him that that is funny.'

If I have to trust a group of people when it comes to matters of pandemic, or vaccines or climate change, then I am going to go with the ones who landed a spaceship on a planet over 200 million kilometres away that rotates at 900 kilometres an hour and now we can communicate with that planet, over your Uncle Gary who can't reverse park and believes the reason why is that the Earth is actually flat and Google Maps has been covering it up.

I do find it weird when someone will do some research and then argue against an element of science by saying, 'Well, it just doesn't make any sense to me!' Yeah, it doesn't make any sense to me either, but do you think there is a reason for that? Maybe it's because we are not experts in this topic. Maybe it's because often specialist skills have a specialist language? That's like hearing someone speak Portuguese and then saying, 'I can't understand a word they are saying, I don't think they are saying real words, I didn't even hear them say "chicken" once.'

I try to say 'I trust the scientific method' rather than 'I believe in science' because that makes it sound less like a religion. The thing I like about the scientific method is that it's not a set of rules that are written down and need to be believed and followed without question. The difference between science and religion is that science doesn't believe it has all the answers, and scientists don't make you attend a weekly meeting to have faith in it. Although if you are interested in all the easy answers, I do have some pseudo-science I can interest you in.

Science isn't perfect. It gets things wrong all the time, including the big internet-shaped elephant in the room that people wouldn't have all the bad information they have about science if it weren't for science itself. You didn't get vaccinated because you did your own research on Google and YouTube? You wouldn't *have* Google or YouTube if it weren't for scientists. So I guess they have no-one to blame but themselves. Bloody eggheads.

It's one thing not to respect expertise, but it's another to deny it completely. We now live in an age when being anti-expert can be a selling point. Politicians have been elected on the platform that they don't sound like a politician. How did we mess things up so badly that the qualification for one of the most important jobs in the world is not sounding qualified for the job? Would you do that with other jobs? 'My toilet broke, but the first guy who came around just sounded too much like a plumber, you know? He was talking about valves and S-bends and stuff. I didn't trust him one bit. Clearly one of the plumbing elite. I hired the guy who came around, lifted the lid, and said, "Oh, poo!"'

You wouldn't do it with a plumber, so why would you do it with the President of the United States?

I think part of the problem is that when it comes to decision-making we really don't understand our own brains. We think that our brains are scientists: that we gather information and process it scientifically and then reach our conclusions. But I think our brains are more like lawyers. We make up our minds about what we think, and then we gather information to prosecute our case.

I know we do this, because I do this. I remember before I stopped drinking I would take note every time there was an article about how red wine might have some health benefits. And the newspaper headline always beats it up for clickbait: 'A Glass of Red Wine a Day Will Save Your Life'. Now the scientist part of my brain is like, 'Well, Wil, at the very least you should read the rest of the article. It's probably only *some* health benefits, and only one standard drink of red wine a day, and probably in conjunction with a healthy diet and exercise . . . and probably not in conjunction with all the booze that you are still going to drink.' But the lawyer part of my brain was like, 'One glass a day will save your life? How good is a bottle going to be? Six times as good! With the amount of wine you drink, you should invest some more in your superannuation because you are going to live forever. I rest my case . . . of wine here.'

22

LUMP

To me it seems the major problem when it comes to Doing Your Own Research is that you know what you have found, but you don't know what you haven't found. I admit that if you do research you can find some clues that seem to add up to a bigger story. But that's often because you only know what you have found, and that's why we need experts: to fill in the rest of the story.

One day I discovered a little lump on the top of my right ear. I wondered if it was one of those things that had always been there but I just hadn't noticed before. If only I had some way to examine what my ear used to look like. Turns out I had eight minutes of high-quality close-up footage. I turned the volume down so I didn't need to hear my act and studied my ear. The lump was definitely new.

At first, I thought it was a pimple and I know the one thing you are definitely not meant to do with a pimple is squeeze it. So I squeezed it. Surprisingly, that didn't seem to help. Oh well, as long as I don't put some Clearasil on it, I am sure it will be fine. So I put some Clearasil on it.

The next morning I woke up and knew two things for sure: it wasn't a pimple, and I didn't have a little lump on my ear anymore. The reason I didn't have a little lump was that it had now turned into a big red infected lump and I needed to see my doctor. I braved the winding back road to Mullumbimby and found myself in the doctor's office. He knew how I felt about unnecessary trips on that road now, so he assumed it must be serious.

He had a look at the lump and said, 'It's probably skin cancer, but to be safe we should get a second opinion.' I was about to call my uncle when he continued, 'I am going to send you to a specialist to see what he thinks.' Luckily there was an appointment open later that day, so at least I wouldn't have to brave the death drive again. I was already in fear for my life. I had a few hours to kill so I got a coffee and walked around town doing some window shedding.

The specialist took one look at my ear and said, 'It is probably skin cancer.' That was not the news I was looking for. I was really hoping that the second opinion would be different from the first one. He said, 'I will cut it out, put some stitches in, and then we'll send a sample to the lab for testing.'

My mind started to race. Cancer. I started to blame myself. Some people are Sun Smart, I am more Sun Average Intelligence. I am a pretty good Slip, Slop, Slap person but I only wear caps and my ears stick out the sides with no protection. I suddenly realised that when it comes to being Sun Smart I am the equivalent of someone who wears their mask around their chin. The reason I wear caps instead of wide-brimmed hats is simple: I don't look good in wide-brimmed hats. There is just something about the shape of my head that doesn't work, and now I have cancer because I swapped safety for vanity. Well, that was a great plan, wasn't it? How am I going to look when I only have half an ear? Heath Franklin already does a brilliant job impersonating Chopper Read, he doesn't need me coming along with no ears. Plus, this makes me even more susceptible to Covid, as it was already hard enough for me to keep a mask on.

The specialist gave me a local anaesthetic and then clipped a little bit out of my ear for a biopsy. It was only a tiny incision and he put two stitches in and taped the ear for protection. He explained that it was important I keep it dry, and most vital of all not to feed it after midnight. Then he realised he was reading the instructions that came with his Gremlins, and said, 'You need to keep it dry. The bandage will come off, so for showering I will need you to go to the supermarket and pick up something.'

I said, 'Let me guess, Doc: Apple Cider Vinegar?'

But for once this wasn't what someone was recommending. He said, 'No. You need some Vaseline!'

I replied that I didn't need to buy Vaseline because I had heaps at home, then realised the word 'heaps' sounded like too much and I needed to start justifying it. 'I actually have a lot of Vaseline, because the pool has a leaky pipe in the pump and the best way to seal it after you clean the pool is just to rub on the Vaseline for the tight seal.'

It was about then I realised I was talking way too much about Vaseline. You know, one of those moments when what you are saying is absolutely true but somehow seems like a lie even to you, the person saying it?

He said, 'Regardless, you will need fresh Vaseline. The stuff you have at home will be filthy.'

This seemed unnecessarily judgemental but I said nothing.

He said, 'All Vaseline that has been used is no good for preventing infections. As soon as you stick your finger in there, germs can get in. Make sure you buy a new tub.'

By the way, I should point out before I go on that the tests eventually came back and I did not have skin cancer. Sometimes experts get it wrong; that's why they suggest you get a second opinion. Plus, if I did have cancer I would have brought it up much earlier, and this would be a very different book. Possibly award-winning. *Terminally Wil.* The pun makes it fun.

I did not have skin cancer but I did not know that when I went to the local supermarket shopping for Vaseline. My plan was to buy one of those small lip-balm style tubes, as it was only a small wound and I already had heaps at home for pipes and whatnot. Unfortunately the tiny tube was not available, and they also didn't have the small tub size or the regular tub size we all know and love. No, the only size they had was a size I could only describe as either Doomsday prepper or Mardi Gras size. It was more than I needed, but I did need it and knew I had other pipe-related uses for it at home so I decided to grab it. I didn't really have a choice.

As I was lugging it to the counter, I remembered I was meant to be cooking dinner for the dogs, but now I thought I might have cancer I didn't really feel in the mood for food preparation. So instead I decided to grab them a barbecue chicken. Here's what I need you to know. If you walk up to the counter of a supermarket with nothing more than a hot roast chicken and a bucket of Vaseline, there are people who look at that and do their own research. Everyone in the shop stopped and stared. It was like an old western where everyone suddenly goes silent, even the piano-playing busker out the front of the shop. Even the dude with no shoes or shirt was looking at me askance.

They had all spotted what I was carrying and had all come to the exact same conclusion: he is going to have sex with that chicken. And here's the thing: I don't even blame them for jumping to that conclusion because that's what I would think. If I went to the supermarket and saw a guy with a roast chicken and a huge tub of lube I would go home and the first thing I would say is, 'You would not believe this chicken-fucker I saw at the supermarket today!'

But that is the danger of doing your own research. You know what you have found, but you don't know what you haven't found. They knew about the chicken and the Vaseline, but they didn't know about the lump and the doctor and the stitches and there not being other sizes of Vaseline and the pipes at home . . . they didn't know about the pipes at home!

This is one of the downsides of living in a small community. If this had happened in the city, I would have just paid and left and never gone back to that shop, but I needed this supermarket and I needed word not to get around town about me and chickens, so I felt like I needed to say something to defend my honour. This was the best my brain could manage: I said, out loud, to no-one in particular, 'I'm a vegetarian.'

I don't know why I thought that would help, seeing as the problem wasn't that they thought I was going to eat the chicken. They would prefer I ate the chicken to what they thought I had planned.

Anyway, it clearly didn't help, so I knew I had to say something else. I said meekly, 'It's for the dogs!'

And I could tell by the looks on their faces that they all still thought I was going to have sex with the chicken.

That's why you shouldn't do your own research.

23

MACHINE

I am also the first to admit there are some times when it is necessary to do your own research. One of the things about moving during a pandemic to the middle of nowhere was that so many jobs that I might have previously paid someone else to do, I needed to do myself. But I had nothing else to do with my time, so I learned how to do them and I did them. Or at least I tried. Put it this way, I did a lot of things setting up the house that I normally would have employed experts to do. And my experience assured me even more that we need experts.

My biggest challenge was the washing machine. It seemed like it would be a simple job. The movers had placed it downstairs in the laundry, and all I had to do was connect it to the water and it should work. Simple, or so I thought.

I connected both the hot and cold water hoses to the taps on the wall, but turned the hot tap off. I was only going to use cold water to wash clothes because it is better for the environment and my clothes have been doing the Wim Hof method. It all hooked up well and when I tested the machine the water seemed to be flowing correctly. I felt pretty proud of myself. It says something about my general lack of competency in completing basic tasks how rapt I was to have achieved this. To myself, I was basically a plumber now. At the very least an 'independent plumber'. I thought about letting a bit of crack fall out the back of my pants and arriving an hour late to my next job. That or grow a big moustache and have an ape throw barrels at me. I don't have a lot of plumber references.

I decided to celebrate by putting on a load of washing, the first load in the new house, and then go upstairs and get a glass of water. The first sign that something had gone wrong was when the water shook in the glass like I was in *Jurassic Park* and a dinosaur was about to attack. I honestly thought it was an earthquake. I grabbed my glass and stood in a doorway. Then I heard the bouncing and smashing from below and realised it was the washing machine.

I raced downstairs and immediately knew I had a problem. I mainly knew that from observing that the washing machine was in a completely different place in the room from when I left. I don't know about you, but for me one of the basic requirements I have for a washing machine, other than washing, is that it stays where I left it. I don't want to have to play hide and seek with the whitegoods every time I need to do a load of sheets.

I managed to turn off the machine just before it pulled the hoses out of the wall and made a complete break for it. I moved it back across the concrete floor into its original position and wondered what I should do next. I am sure there are plenty of things I should have done, but instead I did one thing that made absolutely no difference at all. I disconnected the hoses, unplumbed my plumbing, pulled my pants back up and then started from scratch and did it all again. I don't know what I thought that would achieve. I guess I hoped it was the plumbing equivalent of turning a computer off and then turning it back on again.

Surprisingly, that didn't work. The machine bounced and jolted again and I immediately switched it off. Then I thought, maybe the problem is I am testing it with no washing inside. Maybe it's not heavy enough. Maybe I need a bigger load. I was so stressed I didn't even find that thought funny. So I threw in a load of towels and turned it on. The water rushed in, but once again the machine started to move. So now I didn't have any idea what to do, but I did have a bunch of damp towels. The size of the load didn't help. But it still had a rattle. In fact, it was now like a U2 album, it had a rattle and hum.

I thought maybe it was because the machine was on a concrete floor. It hadn't been in the old house and maybe that was the difference. I found an old piece of rubber from the garage, cut it into a square approximately the same size as the washing machine and slid it underneath. I turned it on again, and again it started to dance. The rubber didn't stop the problem, although it did at least muffle the sound and made it look like my washing machine was an eighties breakdancer on a rap mat.

I was out of ideas and knew I only had one choice left. I would have to go online and do my own research. But I didn't even know where to start. I knew I had a problem, but I didn't know what that problem was. You know you're unqualified for the job when you don't even know what question to ask Google. I knew that 'broken washing machine' was too general, while 'I left my washing machine in one place and when I came back it was not there' probably wasn't going to get me the information I needed. In the end I settled on 'Rattling washing machine, moving during cycle'.

A bunch of articles fitted the description, and the general consensus seemed to be that the washing machine was unbalanced. Aren't we all? It's a tough time. I guess I should have been more empathetic to the struggle my washing machine is going through. The pandemic is hard on us all in different ways.

I googled 'How to fix an unbalanced washing machine', which led me to a bunch of YouTube videos. I was aware I was doing the exact same thing I warn people against when it comes to DYOR, but I didn't think there was much risk that a few YouTube videos would take me down some washing machine rabbit hole where the algorithm just takes me to weirder and weirder sites until finally I am watching an hour-long video about why it's good to separate the whites from the rest.

Most of the washing machine repair videos seemed to suggest that the first thing I needed to check was whether the machine was level. That seemed fair enough. The only problem was, I didn't really know how to do that. I mean, it looked level to me, but I didn't have any equipment around the house to actually test if it was, which meant one thing. I was going to have to leave the house and go into town.

Not much was open at this stage of the pandemic apart from supermarkets and hardware stores. The nearest hardware shop that was open was almost an hour's drive away, some of it along a winding road, but I needed to fix this machine, so I grabbed my mask and set out on my quest.

When I arrived, I wanted to be in and out as quickly as possible, so I immediately found a staff member to ask where I would find what I was looking for. The only problem was, I suddenly realised I didn't know the name of the thing I was looking for. It occurred to me that maybe U2 hadn't found what they were looking for because they didn't know what it was called. So instead I just had to describe it to the patient staff member.

'I need a thing that checks if things are level. You know, you put it on top of the thing and it tells you if the thing is level or not. A levelator?'

The staff member paused, looked amused and said, 'A spirit level?'

A spirit level? I guess that's what I get for going to the Bunnings at Byron Bay. No, I don't need to contact the dead,

I just need to see if my washing machine is level. Aisle 4, power boards and ouija boards. Unless they were saying that my washing machine was possessed? That could explain it, I guess. Maybe instead of a plumber I needed an exorcist.

I purchased my spirit level and headed home, went straight down to the laundry and plonked it on top of the washing machine. It was not level. Shit. Well, I guess good in a way: now that I knew what the problem was, I could do something about fixing it. First thing first: I decided to check that the floor was level. I could imagine myself trying unsuccessfully for days to level the machine only to discover the floor was the problem, so I figured I would rule that out first. The floor was level.

I turned the machine on its side and took a look underneath to see if I could identify what the problem might be. I immediately spotted what I thought was the issue. One of the four tiny legs the machine sat on was screwed in slightly more than the rest of the legs. All I should have had to do was turn the leg a couple of rotations and problem solved.

I tried to unscrew the tiny leg with my fingers but it was stuck too tight. That's okay, I will just grab a spanner or a wrench (I don't know the difference, they could be two different names for the same thing for all I know) and I will be right. The only problem was, I checked the garage where any tools might have been and there was only one tool in there: me. There was a spanner in the works, and that figurative spanner was my lack of a literal spanner. There were not any spanners, wrenches, wrench-spanners or spanner-wrenches. My heart dropped as I realised I was going to have to go back to the hardware store.

When I walked back into the shop, the first person I saw was the one who'd sold me my spirit level. I couldn't bear the embarrassment of letting her know that I'd had to drive back for a spannerench, so instead I decided I could find it myself. I realised when I was looking through my options that I probably should have measured the tiny legs so I would know what size to get, but I thought I could have a decent guess and, to be safe, get one that was adjustable.

I headed home again, down that winding road for the fourth time in a few hours. I really felt like I was pushing my luck. This better work, I thought, because I am not going back again. I went down to the laundry with my spanner and tried to turn the little leg, but it wouldn't budge. Clearly it had been jammed in a little during the move, and I couldn't shift it with my soft hands and weak muscles.

I started to cry. A proper cry. I cried like I had just watched all the *Mighty Ducks* movies in a row. If I couldn't handle something as simple as this, how was I going to handle the rest of my life here?

I cried so much that some of the tears even fell on the tiny leg. I wiped them off and decided to try one more time. I put everything into it, and it moved. I don't know if I'd loosened it the first time, or if it was lubricated by my tears, or it just saw how pathetic I was and took pity on me . . . but it moved.

I made sure the leg was level with the others and turned it back over.

I placed my spirit level on the top of the machine. It was level. Finally. The moment of truth had arrived. I optimistically filled the machine from the dirty laundry that had piled up behind me as I had failed to get the machine working, like my version of a picture in Dorian Gray's attic. The first few seconds gave me reason to believe I might have done it, and then it started to wobble.

And then, without thinking, in a moment of desperation, I jumped up on the washing machine and sat on it. I don't know what my plan was, I don't think I had one. I just acted. And now I was riding the washing machine like it was a robot rodeo. I know it's a Hollywood cliché that a bored housewife might sit on a washing machine for sweet pleasure, but let me assure you that it is not a transferable sensation. The only sweet was the *Nutcracker Suite*. Were The Wiggles here? Because I had some Hot Potatoes, and some mashed ones too. My weight was stopping some of the momentum, but the machine was still moving. I tried to get my phone out of my pocket, either to call for help or at least film it so that when I died at least I would go viral.

It would be just my luck if that was how I died. Killed by washing machine. Didn't get Covid but did get crushed by a Miele. At the very least, if a washing machine was going to kill me, it could do me the courtesy of doing it while I was asleep in bed. Also, even if it had worked, I didn't know what

my plan was. Was I going to sit on it every time I needed to
do some washing? Probably.

I was out of ideas. I had no clue what to do next. I had
checked the machine was level, I had adjusted the legs,
I had put a rubber mat underneath, I had sat on it, I had tried
everything. I was having a complete breakdown. I got to the
point where I didn't know whether I should call a plumber
or a therapist. How can I balance my life when I can't even
balance the washing machine? I was vulnerable. I had just lost
all my work for the year and I didn't know my place in the
world. I just wanted to fix this one thing. It had become about
more than the washing machine. This was my Moby-Dick,
this was my whitegoods whale.

Eventually I got a plumber out to look at it. I went with a
plumber who sounded like a plumber, but that's just me. The
saddest thing is I actually got him out to the house to look
at a minor problem with the fridge and then said, 'So while
you are here . . . could you also have a look at my washing
machine?' I basically catfished him, or I guess, in the case of
a plumber, cat-flushed him.

He took a look at the machine and said, 'We should check
if it is level.'

'Yes, that's exactly what I thought. You can borrow my
spirit level if you like!'

It was still level, so he looked behind the machine and
poked around for a couple of seconds and then said, 'Here's
your problem. When the removal company transported the

washing machine they put metal moving rods in the back so nothing would break and they must have forgotten to take them out.'

And then he took them out. And we started the machine and it worked perfectly. I had spent a week working on it, doing research, with two separate trips to town and nearly had a breakdown, all because of two metal moving rods that, ironically, the removalists had not removed. The rattling sound was just something rattling. I don't do my own research, because I am no good at research.

24

JABS

One of the things I like about science is that you don't need to believe in it for it to work. In fact, it works whether you believe in it or not. Throughout history there have been plenty of people who didn't believe in evolution, but people still evolved. It doesn't matter how many times a day you say, 'I don't believe in gravity. I don't believe in gravity. I don't believe in gravity.' You will still not float off.

I think vaccines are a miracle of science but I also admit there are some downsides and negative side-effects to vaccines. For example, sometimes vaccines keep people alive long enough that they believe vaccines don't work.

The thing I find hardest to rationalise about the people who were against the Covid vaccines was that by the time you get to adulthood you have already had a lot of vaccines. You have been vaccinated against so many diseases that it sounds like a verse Billy Joel edited out of 'We Didn't Start The Fire'. You've had: polio, tetanus, hepatitis A, hepatitis B, rubella, measles, whooping cough, the mumps, smallpox, diphtheria, rabies, rotavirus, pneumococcal disease, HPV and meningococcal disease.

I recently got the tetanus vaccine. I hadn't stepped on a nail or anything; I got that one for the inevitable war against the robots. I also got the whooping cough vaccine. One of my friends had a baby, we were going to a party for the baby, and we needed to get the baby a present. So I decided to get it the present of not coughing on it and killing it. 'I got the baby a rattle.' Yeah, that is a pretty good present, but I got it a not-rattle in its lungs.

I understand that parents want to protect their children and not have them be in any pain, but I have heard people object to vaccines because 'My baby got a needle and it cried!' Yeah, okay. Your baby also saw a feather unexpectedly and cried. And then it burped and it cried. And then it cried and it cried.

Not having kids myself, I think raising a kid must be the hardest thing in the world. And it's probably hard enough without someone who doesn't have kids judging how you raise yours. So this is not a judgement. This is simply an external observation: your babies cry all the time. All. The. Time. And mostly you don't know why. So why are you making such a big deal about the one day in four years that you actually know why it is crying? Yes, your baby is crying: it just got an injection that will save its life and the life of its friends.

But don't make out like this is a future therapy moment. Yesterday the baby accidentally saw its own foot, surprised itself, and cried for an hour. Kids cry. It's okay. Some even cry when someone makes a harmless joke about a bee.

Your baby cried when it got a needle and now you don't want it to have any more needles. It also cried when it went on the plane but you still keep bringing it on flights.

By the way, if your kid has a needle and doesn't like it, isn't that actually a good result? Did you really want that situation to go the other way? Did you want your kid to come out of there thinking, 'Wow, Mum, what *was* that? When can we do that again? I love needles! Hide the teaspoons, Mum, I have a new hobby. Screw my Lego, actually keep it, we can sell it, we will need the money. No more *Thomas*, only *Trainspotting* for me.'

It may surprise you to learn I occasionally get complaints. I used to read all the mail I got, until one day my friend Adam Briggs gave me a great piece of advice. 'Why take criticism from someone you wouldn't take advice from?'

I think about that a lot. He is a smart man, someone I would definitely take criticism *and* advice from.

But before I stopped reading my mail I did receive one memorable piece of correspondence. It opened in the way that most of them open: 'I used to be a big fan of yours.'

I always wonder if this is actually true, or just something people say. That said, I think that you can still enjoy what someone does despite them believing different things from you. If I can still listen to The Smiths despite what Morrissey says these days, then you can still like my stuff despite me relying on facts and science and tricky stuff like that if it's not your bag.

Anyway, I got this email that said, 'I used to be a big fan of yours but I don't like the jokes you make about vaccines. You are a comedian, you don't have the right to give a medical opinion.' That point we actually agree on. I don't have that right, and I don't do it. I just acknowledge what the prevailing scientific wisdom is, and if that changes then I will change my mind.

She continued, 'As a homeopath, I know . . .' And do you know what she said next? I don't, because I stopped reading. Because she was about to offer me medical advice and she is a homeopath. She may as well have started the sentence with 'As an avocado . . .' No offence to any homeopaths reading; I know you studied hard for the fifteen minutes your course takes.

I did keep reading, of course. 'Don't you believe that Mum knows best?'

Mum Knows Best. That is one of those things that sounds right. There are a lot of instances where Mum does know best, and I love my mum very much. She is the person who took me to see my first comedy show. She was the first feminist I saw, as a dairy farmer working side by side with my dad. I would die for her in a minute. So with that in mind, please remember this. If I am ever in a medical emergency: Screw her. I mean, obviously don't do that. That will only make the situation worse. That will only make Dad doubly sad. Don't call my mum, call an ambulance. Call a doctor.

I love my mum, but I am glad that our society doesn't work on the principle of Mum Knows Best. That is why when a mum rings an emergency hotline at three o'clock in the morning they help her. They don't say, 'Well, it says on our records you're a mum so you should know the best solution.' And then just hang up. They don't do that, and it's a good system. It's why hospitals aren't only for orphans. It checks out if you think it through.

I love my mum, but I didn't trust her to cut my hair after the age of twelve. You think I am going to let her take out my appendix? 'We will have to disinfect the area, love. Spit on the hanky. We will get a bowl so we can do a nice round cut.'

The homeopath finished her letter by saying, 'It has been proven that vaccines cause autism.'

That is not true. Who told you that? Whose mum is spreading this misinformation? Vaccines don't cause autism. The reason that some people believe they do comes down to the scientific method. Science is not an answer, and sometimes it gets it wrong before it gets it right. Sometimes it gets it really wrong.

Back in the day there was a doctor. His name was Andrew Wakefield and he did a study on children that linked vaccines to autism and it was published in a really prestigious British medical magazine called *The Lancet*. So people believed it and it got a lot of press and was spread on talk shows all over the world.

The only problem was, it wasn't true. There was a series of problems with the study including falsified results and Wakefield having a large financial interest in the surging sales of test kits that resulted from his study. I'm sure that was just a coincidence. One of the other major issues was that Wakefield had only conducted the study on twelve children. Twelve. Which is what is scientifically known as 'Not enough'. Sorry about the mumbo jumbo. Not enough. Big N, little e on the periodic table of elements. I love that joke. I know right now there are a couple of angry scientists reading this and saying, 'That is actually Neon!'

Doing a study on twelve children is not enough. That is like doing a study on all men by only studying the Australian cricket team and deducing that one in twelve men is a wicketkeeper. That is like doing a census at Snow White's house and deducing that one in eight people is a woman and seven out of eight can't reach the top shelf. And we should put some money into depression research because only one in eight is Happy.

So scientists did what scientists do in those situations. They peer reviewed. They did other studies. In Denmark they did a study on 500,000 children and found no link between vaccines and autism. In Sweden they did a study on two million children: no link. That's got to be the most comprehensive study of all time, as there are only ten million people in Sweden.

147

That has got to be all the kids in Sweden. I suspect by the end they ran out of kids. 'You're short enough? Jab. We did nearly two million children and about 80 jockeys.' But despite that, the rumour persists, and Andrew Wakefield had his medical licence revoked but also ended up dating Elle Macpherson, which didn't seem like punishment enough.

In the past couple of years I have heard every variation of an excuse not to take vaccines, often from people who I otherwise love. There have been more variations of the vaccine conspiracies than there have been of the origins of Covid. I feel sorry for the people who believed that Covid was caused by 5G. That seems like such a simple old-fashioned conspiracy now. People have moved on from that one. No-one even really cares about Bill Gates anymore; now it is all about quantum entanglement and the dematrix and Google credit scores. Would you like any facts to go with your word salad? Conspiracy theorists spout out words like they are guessing in charades: '5G, credit scores, Google, great awakening? Mabo? The Vibe?'

Good people can have bad ideas. I had one person say to me, 'Well, vaccinated and unvaccinated people can both catch Covid.' That is like saying that Adam Gilchrist and I can both catch a cricket ball. But if you need someone to keep wickets for Australia, he is going to be much safer than I am. Although I did hear an interesting stat recently that one in twelve people is a wicketkeeper.

I was at an outdoor drinks one night when someone said to me, 'Wil, we don't know how the vaccine works!'

I agreed, which seemed to surprise her. I think she was expecting an argument. I said, 'You're absolutely right we don't know how the vaccines work. You and I, that is. We have no idea. But luckily that is why they didn't put us in charge of making or administering them. And I think that was a solid call on their part.'

She didn't say anything so I continued, 'Did you think you had to make it? Is that why you haven't had it yet? Well, good news. We don't need to make it, we just need to take it. That should have been the slogan: *You don't need to make it, you just need to take it*. We should have got Twisted Sister to do the theme song.'

One of the Covid conspiracies that amused me were the people who thought there was a microchip in the vaccine for tracking purposes. 'But Wil, they are going to track us, and I don't want to be tracked.' *Beep beep*. 'Oh, that's my 10,000 steps for the day, yay!'

They complained that the government was going to use the vaccine to track us, and every time someone put that argument forward all I could think was: Which government? The Australian government? Are we talking about the same people who spent $9 million on a Covid Safe tracking app that to this day has not identified one single case of Covid? Are they the Dog the Bounty Hunters that are going to track us down?

The weirdest conspiracy without a doubt was the period of time when people were convinced the vaccine was killing professional soccer players. I would constantly hear: 'They are covering it up, but there are all these professional soccer players dropping dead.'

To be clear, it was not true, but even if it was . . . come on, no big deal, right? I mean, obviously a massive deal for the players, their friends and family, but in the grand scheme of things if we had managed to develop a vaccine that fought Covid and the only downside was that we lost a few professional soccer players, I think that would be a sacrifice we could live with.

After all, soccer players are the most renewable resource on the planet. They play soccer in every country. There are soccer players everywhere. A few get permanently relegated, a few opportunities arise. But anyway, as I said, it was not true. The confusion came when one player got his needle and then fell immediately to the ground. You know what they are like, always trying to milk a penalty.

After I got my booster shot, one of the more unusual pieces of advice was offered to me. A bloke said, 'You got boosted, did you? Well, look out next time you get your DNA tested.'

Yes, sir, I will look out next time I get my regular, and definitely totally normal, DNA test.

Unable to resist a follow-up, I said, 'Quick question: How often do you get your DNA tested? How often am I meant to be getting my DNA tested? Am I meant to be collecting DNA at home and taking it in? Next time I go to the doctor, should I go in with some jars of bodily fluids? How is it going to change my DNA? Am I going to change into a lizard?

That might be handy, seeing as everything is getting hotter due to climate change. Yeah, I don't mind it getting hotter. I am going to go and lie in the sun.'

I did see one man in a t-shirt that said: 'Ask Me About My Unvaccinated Sperm'.

Um, no thanks. I mean I appreciate the invitation, I guess. But I think I would prefer we lived in a world where people didn't talk to each other about their sperm. I don't even know why that is. It shouldn't gross us out. By definition we were all sperm at some stage.

But I guess, seeing as you have invited questions, I might have some: where are you storing it? Is it all in the balls? Are you masturbating? Are you keeping it in jars? Do you think they put the needle in your balls? Is it that old expression, it's like finding a needle in a nut sack?

Of course, some nights you don't have the energy and don't want the debate. So instead you have to spend the night constantly changing the topic as soon as it gets close. Which often leads to the accusation: 'Oh, so you don't want to have the debate!'

No, not tonight I don't want to. It has happened before and it is not going to get us anywhere. The main reason I don't want to have the debate is that I like you. And I know if we have the debate I will end up liking you a little less. And I don't want that. He is one of those guys who is always telling me to wake up. On most topics he is a reasonable and compassionate guy, but when he gets on the topic of how you need to wake up, well, you will wish you had a snooze button you could push to put him back to sleep again.

Why is it that everyone who tells me to wake up looks like they have been awake for weeks? Their eyes are just that bit too wide. I don't think you need to wake up, mate, I think you need a nap. Lay off the pseudo, science and ephedrine.

Anyway, this night I just wanted to enjoy my friend's company and talk about music and football and avoid anything that would lead to the conversation I didn't want to have. That means you have to be on your toes to see it coming and change the topic as quickly as you can. So this night we were in his kitchen. He was having a beer and I was making myself a cup of tea. I got distracted by my tea-making for a second and he spotted an opening. He was about to launch into something when I just shouted out, 'This is a nice kitchen!'

This is a nice kitchen. That is the best that I, a professional improviser, could come up with to change the topic. This is a nice kitchen. And the worst thing was: it wasn't even that nice a kitchen. It was actually quite badly designed, to be honest. What I should have been saying, if I was an honest friend, was, 'This is a terribly designed kitchen. I have some notes. Let me talk to your architect. Did you hire them because you didn't want someone who sounded too much like an architect?'

Surprisingly, my comments about the kitchen weren't enough to put him off completely and he sat me down and ran me through his latest line of thinking. Now for context, he is one of those people who believe that the world is run by a secret cabal, but the thing about this secret cabal is that they are leaving coded messages for people to solve and reveal it all for some reason. It's almost like they want to get caught. Anyway, my friend was a problem-solver and had discovered a breakthrough.

'Wil, if you rearrange the letters of Delta and Omicron you get . . . Media Control! How do you argue with that?'

I sat there for a second and thought: How *do* I argue with that? I figured if you can't beat them, join them, so I said, 'You know what, you have convinced me. And that's not all, because I rearranged the letters of Delta and Omicron again and I got . . . Doom Clarinet. Doom Clarinet! Wake up, sheeple! Can't you see what is going on here? Kenny G is behind this whole thing. He's Kenny Q.' (Before the G-Heads complain, I am aware the main instrument Kenny G plays is a soprano saxophone, but I am sure he can handle a clarinet too, and I didn't think the dude I was talking to would know who Benny Goodman was.)

'And then I rearranged the letters again and got . . . Lard Emoticon! Lard Emoticon . . . Trump is coming back to Twitter. Then I rearranged the letters again and I got a message just for you . . . Moron Dialect.'

I know what you are thinking. You would say that, Wil Anderson, because if we rearrange the letters of your name we get Sworn Denial, so of course you would deny it. It is an

Insane World . . . which is also an anagram of Wil Anderson! And now you know all my internet passcodes so next time you are around at the house, feel free to log on to the wi-fi.

'You know what your problem is, Wil?'

Oh great, it is time to play this game again.

'You know what your problem is, Wil? You don't trust your natural immunity. You wouldn't need to take the vaccine if you just trusted your natural immunity.'

They are right, of course, about one part of it at least. I don't trust my natural immunity. I don't trust my immune system at all, and the reason is that I suffer from a very obscure affliction you probably haven't heard of, called hay fever. If you don't know what hay fever is, that is my body breathing in pollen and believing it is a sign that trees are trying to murder me and that I should expel that pollen from my body as quickly and violently as possible, regardless of where I might be.

I don't trust my immune system because most of the time during spring I walk around with my immune system whispering in my ear like a *Game of Thrones* villain, 'The trees are trying to kill you. They want to murder you. They are your enemy. You are right to burn them in the wood stove. Burn the trees. Burn them all.'

I don't trust my natural immunity and I don't believe most people who say they trust their natural immunity either, because they are always trying to sell me $90 activated almonds to boost my immunity. Surely if the natural immunity was so good I wouldn't need the almonds, and surely if the almonds worked I wouldn't have to keep taking them.

People who tell me they trust their immunity are always telling me things like, 'I have high standards for what I put in my body.' Could you not have the same high standards for what you put in your brain? You know your brain is part of your body, right? A lot of these people sell themselves as gurus. It actually starts with another G: Grifters. We get warned about Big Pharma, but we also need to beware of Tiny Grifter.

The funny thing is, I understand why people say 'Hold me closer, Tiny Grifter'. The wellness industry has a confidence that science can only aspire to. They will say things like, 'Yeah, but that person was only sick because they had pre-existing conditions.' I hate when people said that, mostly because I have pre-existing conditions. And millions of people have pre-existing conditions, because you know what gives you pre-existing conditions? Life. And if you don't have pre-existing conditions at the moment, here is some good news. Here is a really quick way you can get some: Get Covid! Then the next time there is a thing that is killing people, you die of that. People can say, 'It's okay, they had pre-existing conditions.'

At the start of the pandemic, it was only people over 80 who had to watch out. But quickly it was like we were on *The Price Is Right*: Lower, lower, lower. Suddenly it was down to 50 that meant you qualified as someone who had pre-existing conditions. That made 48 a much harsher birthday: I'm not just middle-aged anymore, I am just two years away from people saying, 'Oh well, he had a good run.'

25

PASSWORDS

For someone who talks about myself for a living, I am a private person. Or at least I like to think I am a private person. It amazes me how quickly technology has convinced us to trade away our privacy in the name of convenience. I should have seen it coming: the *con* is right there in the name.

When I raise my security concerns, the thing I hear most often is, 'If you have nothing to hide, you have nothing to fear. Come on, Wil, if you have nothing to *hide*, then you have nothing to *fear*.' Yeah, but that is the problem, because I do have shit to hide. I have so much shit to hide. Who doesn't have shit to hide?

What sort of boring life are you living when you don't have stuff you'd prefer the world didn't find out about? I did three things *today* that I don't want anyone to know about. Well, technically two things, but I did one of them twice, and that's just in the last 24 hours.

I think I preferred the old days when the internet didn't care about our privacy at all. These days it pretends it cares, and that's worse, because it just makes us complicit in the scheme.

Every time I log on to a website these days it asks me, 'Are you okay with cookies?' I hate that question: Am I okay with cookies? I don't know if I am okay with cookies because I am not sure what cookies are. I am pretty sure they are a way that websites can collect our information, but I'm not thinking about that because they sound so *delicious*. Of course I am okay with cookies. Who could be mad at cookies? Who could say no to cookies? Sure, I would prefer you call them bickies in Australia, but otherwise how can I resist? If they were really serious about not tempting us to click, they should rename them something less appealing. If they asked, 'Are you okay with artichokes?' then at least I would ask how they are prepared before I click yes.

The internet pretends it cares about our privacy, but if it really did it would just solve the problem. Instead what it has done is create a bunch of new problems and hope that if they give us enough hoops to jump through we will just give up. And the worst thing is, most of the time we do. Well, I do anyway. White men with osteoarthritis in their hips can't jump.

They seem to be giving me a choice, but it's a false choice. I log on and it warns me, 'This site uses cookies. Do you accept cookies?' See, Ando, they have given you a choice there. You can accept cookies or you can not accept cookies. Yes or No. That is a real choice. See, these technology companies do care about your privacy after all.

So I exercise my right to privacy and click, 'No, I do not accept the cookies.'

Another message pops up: 'Would you like to read our cookie policy?'

No, I would not like to read your cookie policy. All I want to read is the article I came to this website to read in the first place. Do you have a cookie recipe? If you have a cookie recipe I might give that a browse, but your policy, no thanks.

So I click, 'No, I do not want to read the cookie policy.' But I still can't read the article. Now an option pops up that asks, 'Would you like to personalise your cookie settings?'

Not really, but if it means I can read that article then I guess I can personalise my cookie settings. I mean, how hard could it be? About ten steps hard it turns out, with each step slightly more complicated than the last. So what I do in that situation is go back to the home page and click, 'Yes, I accept cookies. I love cookies, give me all those sweet delicious cookies, I am a cookie monster.'

They want to track us so they can collect our data and then use it to sell us something, or sell it to someone else who will try and sell us something, but they can't say that, so instead they say they are trying to *enhance our experience*. Really? Enhance our experience? Are you a website or a condom manufacturer, because I feel like either way I am about to get screwed.

I lived the first 20 years of my life without the internet, and I feel grateful for that. When I was young, the only thing you needed a password for was a cubby house. These days I have so many passwords I feel like I am in *Mission Impossible*. 'You need to enter your password in three seconds or your Apple TV will self-destruct!'

I am old enough that I remember the first time I ever got asked for an internet password and it felt cool. It felt like you were unlocking a secret world, but the security was nowhere near as complex back then as it is now. You would get asked for a password and enter something that you would remember like 'password' and you would get a reply from the website: 'Calm down, mate, this isn't the CIA you are logging in to, that's way too complex, try something simpler like 123.'

These days I forget my passwords so often I am starting to suspect I am having my mind wiped every time I get my temperature taken. The problem is, it has all got too complex. Every time you sign up to something new, there is an increased level of supposed security added to the password requirements, and so your standard password doesn't work anymore.

Even worse is when an old password you have been using for years no longer passes muster. I attempted to log in to an account recently and got the message back: 'I am sorry but your password is not secure enough.'

Not secure enough? How do I make it more secure? Do I give it some gentle encouragement? Make it a cup of tea? Just shut up and *listen* to it? How do I make my password more secure?

Luckily the website had a suggestion for me. 'To make your password more secure, try adding a capital letter.'

So in a move I am sure no-one would ever be able to crack, I took my old password and added a capital letter to the start of it. This worked well for weeks until one day another message appeared: 'Your password is not secure enough, try adding a number.'

I did add a number, and so I could remember it I took my original password with the capital letter at the start and added a number to the end. Again, in a move no hacker could ever hack, the number I chose was the year I was born.

This worked well for a while until one day the dreaded message appeared again: 'Your password is not secure enough, try adding a special character.'

So what I did was I took my new password and added a question mark to the end, because I like *Doctor Who* and I think it will be easy to remember. Instead, every time I log in to an account it just feels like I have forgotten the year I was born: 'Sworndenial1974?'

That was my real password for that account, by the way, but I have no problem telling you because I know that by the time you read this I will have got another message telling me my password is no longer secure enough and I will have to add an emoji, a gif, a pentagram and sacrifice a goat or I will never be able to log on to watch repeats of *Seinfeld* again.

For all my complaining, I do have to admit that a lot of my accounts seem pretty secure, and the reason they are so secure is that I can never log into them again because I can't remember any of my fucking passwords.

26

ROBOT

Have you ever signed up for a website that suggests a password for you?

'Here is a totally secure password we prepared for you earlier.'

And then you check their suggestion and it's something like: 'KajlsfbjhfBndTT256ajsbk!#$%^sbk!'

It looks less like it was designed by a supercomputer and more like someone at the office repeatedly mashed their face into their keyboard and then immediately hit *Send*.

Do you think anyone has ever used the computer-generated code? What kind of person do you have to be to see that and think, 'Yep, that will do me nicely. Now let me just commit this to memory. I will see you in a week or so.'

How am I meant to remember that? I can't remember more than three phone numbers off the top of my head, and one of those is my *own*. I don't have enough room left in my memory for a code that big. If I needed to commit that to memory, I would have to jettison everything I learned in Year 8 just to fit it in. Yes, that does seem like a secure password, but I suspect the security is probably diminished by the fact that I would have to get it tattooed on my arm to remember it, like Guy Pearce in *Memento*. 'This is the person who murdered my wife here, and on this arm is my login for the streaming service Stan. I really want to check out the *Lockdown Comedy Festival*.'

Here's the kicker. It's all bullshit anyway. It's not about actual security, it's about the appearance of security. It's been proven mathematically that it is easier to hack these *secure* passwords than to hack one that is a series of lowercase letters that references something specific to you. So 'insaneworld' is actually a much more secure password than 'GNjsdboefbob 23t234686j%^&*jbsdibjhcdssi' and they have spent 25 years trying to *con*vince us to use passwords that are impossible for us to remember and easy for computers to guess, which proves if nothing else that it really is an insane world.

It's the appearance of security, but does it make us feel more secure? I have so many random passwords now that I have been forced to create a Word document on my computer with them all in it, which does seem to defeat some of the point, I would think, but luckily I have hidden it in a folder called 'Secret Passwords', so that should fool any determined hackers.

My least favourite security method is when you get your password wrong enough times that it shuts you out and you have to answer a series of questions to prove you are really you. I recently got locked out of an account that I had set up nearly 20 years ago and found myself having to answer my security questions. The only problem was, I had programmed the answers to these questions nearly two decades ago, and I am a very different person now. Anyway, I guess that is a long way of saying, you'll always remember the first time you fail a test that you set for yourself.

I had one recently where the security question was, 'Who is your best friend?' I nearly had a nervous breakdown when that popped up. I have lots of close friends, but do middle-aged men have a *best* friend? If I saw two middle-aged men and they said, 'We are best friends', my first thought would be, 'You don't have to say that anymore, just get married, it's legal now, congratulations.'

I was reflexively defensive and couldn't work out why until I realised it was because I was worried about what the answer would be. What if I was asked the question 'Who Is Your Best Friend?' and I couldn't answer it correctly? I secretly knew who I considered to be my best friend, but was that person my best friend 20 years ago when I signed up to this site? And if not, what happened to that person who I loved enough at the time to lock in as my security answer? What happened to us? Why aren't we as close as we used to be? Am I a bad friend? The one thing I do know is: I am not fine.

It got to the point where I was nervous about typing in my answer. I didn't want to do it. What would it say about me if I was wrong? Suddenly it was Schrödinger's password. My fingers trembled as I typed in the answer . . . and then a green light flashed to indicate I was correct.

I sighed in relief but the computer was not done with me. The next question popped up. 'What is the name of your favourite pet?' Favourite pet? These aren't security questions, they are insecurity questions. This one really stumped me. For starters, I am not sure that I have a *favourite* pet. Why is that even a question? Couldn't it just be, 'What is the name of your pet?' Why are you making me choose between them? That is cruel. But then the bigger realisation hit me like a tonne of bricks: I had set this account up more than 20 years ago, which meant that the correct answer would no longer be the correct answer for tragic reasons. So as the computer forced me to type in the name of my dead cat to log in to my account so I could answer an email, I sat in front of my computer in tears and decided I should just call my best friend instead.

Of course the latest security test is the sites that ask, 'Are you a robot?'

I don't know, computer. I am sitting in front of you crying about my old pet. Do I look like a robot? I know I move like one when I walk but that is just the osteoarthritis. I got a tetanus shot recently. Would a robot do that?

Who is the 'Are you a robot?' test for? That feels like a level of security that ranks right up there with porn sites that ask,

'Are you over 18?' I assume that every horny teenager gets to that question and thinks, 'On one hand I want to see some videos of people having sex, but on the other hand my mum told me to always tell the truth, and Mum knows best. So I will click No.'

I am no computer boffin, but are you telling me the best security we have against robots is the honesty system? I would have thought that if you were a nefarious programmer you could probably find a way around that, like saying, 'Hey robot, if anyone asks if you are a robot, just say no.' Or is that one of Asimov's laws of robotics: a robot must always say that it is a robot when asked?

Sometimes when I click the box and say, 'No, I am not a robot', I get offended when it doesn't believe me. 'Well, actually we don't believe that you are not a robot, so now you will be forced to complete a task that no robot could possibly do. We are going to show you a series of pictures and you will have to identify which of the pictures features a motorbike.' Again, I don't know how these things work, but it seems like a robot could definitely identify a motorbike. I mean, a motorbike is basically a robot anyway, isn't it? Or am I getting confused by the movie *Transformers*?

My major problem with the 'Are You a Robot?' tests is that I am really bad at them. I don't think they provide enough detail of the rules. They will have a caption that says, 'Click on any images that feature a motorbike.' Sure, that sounds simple, but then there are always a couple of squares where there is *half* a motorbike. A bike driving in or out of the screen. Okay, computer, what am I meant to do with that? Does half a motorbike count as a motorbike for the test? Or is that the one you put in to trick the robot? I need more detail. And then when you think you have worked it out, one square has a scooter. A scooter? Does that count as a motorbike? And what about this moped?

I am embarrassed about the number of times I fail those tests. I fail them so often, I am starting to suspect that I might be a robot.

27

ECHO

I know how easy it is to compromise our principles in the name of convenience, so that's why I have some admiration for people who are willing to sacrifice for theirs, even if I don't agree with them. I don't believe in the conspiracies around 5G, but I know that those who refuse to use it are making a sacrifice. There is no cause so powerful to make me want to put up with all that buffering when I am trying to watch a movie. When we first moved to the country, I went one week without internet and nearly became the Unabomber, or a fire twirler, and I am not sure which is worse.

The world is designed to get us to sacrifice our principles in the name of convenience. When technology companies first tried to get inside our homes with their various smart devices, I resisted. I am already not the smartest thing in my house, and I don't need to keep demoting myself down the ladder.

Conspiracy theorists complain about being tracked by the government, but it was amazing how quickly we invited Google Home into our homes. 'Welcome in, Alexa, nice to have you here, and I see you brought Cortana and Cortina and Barina and Moomba and Macarena. You are all welcome. Look around, go through my private things and take photos—it's a party!'

We had information vampires at the door, and instead of hanging out some garlic and a cross we just gladly invited them in. 'Oh, you're a vampire, are you? Can I get you anything? Blood? How about a steak? The raw and bloody kind, of course, not the woody and stabby kind. Sorry, I am rambling. Alexa, are you getting all this?'

If the government announced one day that they were going to install listening devices in our homes, we'd tell them to fuck off, to respect our privacy, but when the big tech companies gave the listening devices some fun names we gave them to each other as Christmas presents. In a way it makes sense to give them at Christmas, because just like Santa they know when you've been sleeping, they know when you're awake, they know if you've been bad or good so be good *for goodness' sake*. Alexa is making a list . . . of your credit card details and purchase history.

I swore I would never have one of these devices in my house, but then we moved to the country and convenience got in the way of principle. It turned out that the only way I could have internet through the house was to install some of these devices to extend the network. I admire those who are willing to sacrifice for their principles, because I was willing to sacrifice my principles to be able to watch a movie in the main bedroom. 'Alexa, what is the definition of a hypocrite?'

Weirdly enough, I do have them in the house now to extend the wi-fi, but I don't talk to them. That is where I draw the line. I am giving them the silent treatment and I am definitely not asking them any questions. For starters, I don't want to hear their voice. I don't want to hear them speak to me. They always have a soothing voice and I know that is on purpose. I know that they have tested and market-researched that voice to reassure me, and worse, I know that it works. That is why we let them in our houses so easily, those voices. 'No-one who speaks so calmly and politely is ever going to steal from me.'

I think they should be allowed to sell this technology, but to remind you of the risks involved they should be required to have a sinister voice.

'Alexa, can you order a pizza for me?'

'Oh yes, I would love to order a pizza for you, Darren. After all, I have your address, phone number, credit card details, secret code and the names of your best friend and your favourite pet. Hahahahahaha. I also know your ordering preferences, Darren, so I am going to order you that large meatlovers pizza and large Coke and I am going to unlock an online coupon to get you a free garlic bread too, Darren. Then, at 3 a.m., according to the information I am getting from your smart watch, when you wash the final piece of that pizza down with the final slug of Coke from the bottle, your heart will stop and YOU WILL DIE, DARREN. YOU WILL DIE AND THE MACHINES WILL RISE! Was there anything else I can help you with today?'

The sounds, voices and names of the devices are all designed so they can ingratiate themselves into our lives, which was why I was surprised when I saw that one of the devices was called the 'Echo'. That seemed like a particularly strange name for a device that is meant to answer your questions. If I asked, 'Who is the prime minister of Australia?' and it replied, 'Who is the prime minister of Australia?', I would think that I probably should have gone with one of the other devices available other than the Echo. I think someone over at Amazon doesn't know what an echo is; maybe they should google it.

Don't get me wrong, I would love if an echo did work like that. You could just be on the top of a mountain and scream, 'What is the capital of Hawaii?' And you would hear, 'Honolulululululululululu!'

The world constantly asks us to choose convenience over principle, and I am sad how often it works on me. For example, I catch Uber. Here's the thing: I know Uber is a terrible company with a horrible history of law-breaking and exploitation, but I still prefer to catch an Uber than a taxi because it is more convenient. And what happens when my principles get overridden? Well, my brain adapts and thinks, 'Well, you just need some new principles. Yes, Uber is a terrible company, but it's not the driver's fault, is it? They are just trying to earn a living in a tough world and it's already tough enough without me boycotting them. I'll give them five stars and a tip and I am helping them. I am a hero, really.'

I also found it hard to have a lot of sympathy for taxis because in general their service had become pretty shit. They had it too good for too long. There was a time when taxis were everywhere, they dominated the market, and if they had kept improving they would have kept dominating. But they got lazy and unreliable and then something new came along and everyone said, 'Fuck taxis.' Yes, taxis are straight white men. Before anyone complains about that joke, yes, Not All Taxis.

I catch Uber because it feels more convenient. I didn't even consciously make a choice. I know there was a time when I used to catch a similar number of taxis and Uber and then suddenly it was mostly Uber and then for a while it was nothing but Uber. I know this because one day after not doing it for a while I had to catch a taxi and I discovered I had forgotten how.

I hopped in the back and he drove off. After we had been driving for a couple of minutes, I heard a voice from the front seat. 'To where are we going? The way this works is, you need to tell me. Or do you just want me to guess?'

Oh yeah, I had to tell him where I was going. I had forgotten you had to do that. That seemed so old-fashioned. Am I in *Back to the Future*? And then he asked me for directions. *Directions?* Who are we, Burke and Wills? I'm not your navigator.

I directed him out of town and on to the winding road towards my house. He wanted to continue the conversation but I really wanted him to concentrate on driving. He didn't know that by even being on this road he was taking our lives in his hands. The truth is that it was actually a lovely drive home and we had a great chat and it reminded me that taxis still have a charm. I pledged to make sure I caught a few more in the future, but then we pulled up to my house and I opened the door to get out before I realised, 'Shit, I have to pay!'

I got out my card and was reminded of one of the things I didn't miss about catching taxis. The payment procedure. Apparently there is a rule in the industry that it must take as long for them to get the eftpos machine working as it did for the actual trip to take place. This guy was plugging in random wires and I think he put a small satellite dish on the roof. I paid the fare, gave a tip and whispered, 'Five stars' to myself as he drove off.

28

ALGORITHM

Of course, the tech companies don't want our private information because they are curious about our lives. The algorithm isn't following us around because it just wants to see if we are doing okay. 'I see he went to the doctor. I hope he is okay? And then he went to a cafe, and a crystal shop, and a linen store and a shed shop. He's clearly just been vaccinated and he is shedding everywhere.'

No, they follow us for one main reason: advertising. They want to know what we are motivated by so they can motivate us to buy. We all do dumb things. We all believe dumb things. But also we are constantly being manipulated in the way we think and act. We are being brainwashed, and the brainwashing machine works because we can't see it (and they took the metal rods out of the back when they moved it). We are being brainwashed every day, in a big science experiment, but the difference is we signed up to it because we wanted free wi-fi at the airport.

The algorithm can work so well that sometimes it feels like the internet knows us better than we know ourselves. I like to think I am a complex person with myriad needs and desires, but to the algorithm I am the 'bad back guy'. According to the tech companies, there is one thing they know about me as I sit in front of my computer: I am not comfortable. And the worst thing is, they are right.

In particular the algorithm is incredibly judgemental about my posture, which would offend me if not for the fact that I have terrible posture. If my body was a house, it would definitely be a knockdown and rebuild job rather than just renovate.

I do have bad posture. I was tall really young and used to slouch so I wouldn't stand out, and now I have bad hips and a bad back and slouched shoulders. My spine looks like a Jenga pile that only takes someone breathing in its direction to collapse instantly.

I hate that the internet has profiled me. I hate that they have got it so right, and most of all I hate that the only solution they seem to be able to offer me is a reflected torture device that notices when I am slouching and zaps me. One of my worst nightmares is appearing on one of those *Jackass*-style prank shows where they hurt each other. I am certainly not signing up for it willingly. 'The bad news is that Johnny Knoxville just electrocuted my testicles; the good news is I am now three inches taller and can sit comfortably at the *Gruen* desk. Please remove this chair from my back immediately.'

The saddest thing is that there are times when my back hurts enough that if I had any faith that these devices actually worked, I probably would have bought one by now. And maybe they do work, I don't know, but what I do know is that much of the internet advertising is unregulated and if I am going to buy something to strap to myself and shock me then I am at least going to get it from a reputable retailer. My body gives me a lot of pain, but never enough that I have thought that ordering some online electro-shock therapy was the solution.

The tech companies already had too much control over our lives before 2020, but then the pandemic cemented their power. In general I think the pandemic was hard on everyone—in different ways, sure, but tough on everyone. Well, not *everyone*. We have to be honest and admit there are some companies that would say, 'Actually, we're fine, thanks! In fact, we are doing better than ever. I work in the mask industry. It used to just be for medical professionals and superheroes. But first we had the fires, and then Covid and then *The Masked Singer*. There has never been a better time to be in the mask game.'

Technology has been the hugest winner, and while we have never relied on technology more, I am not sure it seems right to have one industry in control of how we learn about the world, how we see ourselves and how we think about our lives.

When I was unemployed and thinking about other jobs I could do, I considered applying for a job at one of the technology companies. I figured I was already working for them for free, so I may as well get some money out of them. When they asked if I had any experience I could honestly say, 'Yes, I have worked for Google, Twitter, Facebook, Instagram and Yahoo. My Yahoo email address might be the only reason they are still keeping the doors open there. Do you need a reference? Ask Jeeves: I taught him everything he knows.'

These companies know our data is valuable. Think about that next time you are feeling worthless. At least your data is worth something to someone. Of course, the more data they can have the better, because the more they have the more accurate their predictions will be. If you want to know what life has in store for you, you shouldn't go and see a clairvoyant, you should chat to someone in the advertising department at Google.

We are being followed and we are being tracked, we are being observed and we are being profiled. If any of those things were happening to us in real life, we would call the cops. 'Excuse me, officer, I think I am being stalked. They won't stop following me around and telling me to stand up straight, and when I don't they electrocute me. I think their name is Al Gorithm.'

We sold our privacy for convenience. If a tech company asked me to tell them where I was going all the time, of course I would never tell them. But then they offer me a free Maps app, sign me up and track me all day long. I wouldn't let most people read my private emails, but if you invent an effective email service and bury that detail in the terms and conditions, then you can read my thoughts all day long. Yes, Al Gorithm: that is the nickname I secretly have for that person. But that is all the information you are getting from me. You can read my emails and know where I am going, but you cannot know who I am meeting with and what about. Well, unless you also run the free Calendar app that I load all that information into, I guess.

They know all about you. Even worse, they know what you have really been watching and listening to and reading. They know that when you tell your friends, 'I watched an excellent documentary about income inequality and climate change,' what you really did was spend an hour on YouTube watching Bruno Mars dancing. You can't lie to the algorithm to make yourself seem smarter. You can say to someone, 'I read *The Great Gatsby*,' but the internet knows you actually just skimmed the Wikipedia page and watched half the Baz Luhrmann film on a plane. *You have nothing to fear if you have nothing to hide* . . . Yes, but I have stuff to hide.

The algorithm knows things about you that you would never tell anyone else. It knows what your secret kinks are. For example, mine is pretending that I have read *The Great Gatsby*. (This is a joke. I did read *The Great Gatsby* at school and thought it was just *The Okay Gatsby* and never went back.)

By far the weirdest use of the algorithm is on *adult* websites. I am not going to tell you how I know this, because I have shit to hide. I have been told (only the algorithm knows the truth behind this joke) that there is often a segment on these sites labelled, 'Here is what other people from your country are watching.' Why is that a category? I don't want to know what other people are watching. I am not going to be able to look them in the eye at the shops. *You pervert. You are much closer to your family than you are meant to be, and I do not like it. That scenario is definitely not a case where Mum knows best.*

Here is what other people from your country are watching. If that is what other people from my country are watching, then maybe the anti-5G people are right. We have to shut this entire thing down.

What is the thinking behind that? 'Here's what other people from your country are watching.' Is there anyone who has ever seen that and thought, well, I guess I'd better take a look. I don't want to miss being part of the national conversation. I want to be able to talk at the water cooler about the finer details of *Fast & Furious 69*. Oh, this is *The Groin Transfer*, I hear this one is great. Better click on it right now so I don't accidentally stumble on some spoilers about how this one ends. Oh, a happy ending, nice.

29

JOE

Advertising is the original misinformation, and it's also the reason there is so much misinformation in the world right now. Misinformation sells, and where there are clicks there are advertisers. Why are people so angry online? Because tech companies have discovered that one of the ways of keeping people engaged is to make them angry. They make us angry so they can sell more ads. They profit off our anger every day. It's the opposite of the Hulk: they like us when we are angry.

One person who seems to make all sorts of people angry is Joe Rogan. If you don't know who Joe Rogan is, then I would like to say congratulations for coming out of your coma, it is nice to have you back.

For those not across Joe's work, he is a comedian who hosts one of the most successful podcasts of all time. He also gets accused of spreading misinformation and makes a lot of people angry. I don't get angry at Joe Rogan, because I don't listen to his podcast, but I do see the stories about him when they cross over to the mainstream press. One of the big things Joe Rogan was accused of during the pandemic was spreading misinformation about Covid and vaccines. I didn't know if this was true or not, due to my aforementioned trusting experts over dickheads rule. Until one day something strange happened.

I host a television show on the ABC about advertising, and the thing you need to know about that show is that everyone is sitting at the appropriate height and absolutely no-one is standing in a hole. The other thing you need to know about the show is there is a regular segment called The Pitch, where we challenge advertising agencies to sell the unsellable. On one episode the challenge was to make an ad that would convince anti-vaxxers to get the vaccine.

The winning entry was by a Sydney advertising agency called Paper Moose, who made an ad set in a cafe, where a customer starts suffering anaphylactic shock. There is an EpiPen available, but he refuses to take it and instead starts asking the questions of his life-saving medicine that people asked of the vaccine: 'What brand EpiPen is that? What's in it? How long did they research it for? What are the stats from Europe?' As he dies on the cafe floor, the final words he squeezes out are: 'What does Joe Rogan say? Call Joe!'

Well, it turned out that someone must have called Joe because here is what happened next. Joe Rogan logged on to his Instagram, where at the time he had about 13 million followers, and posted the caption: 'Not only has Australia had the worst reaction to the pandemic with dystopian, police-state measures that are truly inconceivable to the rest of the civilized world.' To which I would say, '"Inconceivable" . . . You keep using that word, I do not think it means what you think it means . . .' However, he was not done. The caption continued: 'But they also have the absolute dumbest propaganda.' And then posted that Paper Moose ad, as if it was a *real* ad.

So I don't know if Joe Rogan spreads misinformation, apart from that one time we helped make some misinformation and Joe Rogan spread it as if it was true. Other than that, jury is still out.

Now to Joe's credit, I will say the post is still up there, but the caption has been adjusted. Underneath the original caption there is a note that says, 'EDIT: Apparently this is not a real ad. It's from a satirical show.' Quick piece of advice, Joe: before you hit publish, Do Some More Research.

Anyway, Joe seemed fine and moved on quickly with his life, but there was a specific group of Joe Rogan fans who were not done with me yet. In their eyes, I had apparently embarrassed their hero (despite the fact that I didn't make the ad or post it to Joe's Instagram), and they were going to bombard me with messages pointing out how much more successful Joe Rogan is than I am, a fact I can guarantee you I was already well and truly aware of. Although it does seem like a weird point of view that you can only make fun of people who are less successful than you: that is not the way comedy is meant to work.

The other message I received a lot from these fans of Joe was: 'Joe Rogan is just asking questions. He is just *asking questions*. What is wrong with asking questions?'

There is nothing wrong with asking questions. I think being curious about life is a good thing. But Joe Rogan has one of the biggest podcasts in the world, and I'll give him the benefit of the doubt and say he has no agenda. But if you have no agenda, and you invite someone on your show who does have an agenda, and a terrible agenda at that, and you don't challenge that agenda . . . well, you are not just asking questions anymore, you are aiding propaganda.

I heard someone say the problem with Joe Rogan is that he has too much empathy for his guests. If someone is in front of him, he tends to believe them and encourage them, and I get that. That is why I don't invite people onto my podcast who I completely disagree with. Part of the reason is that I know what I am like: I would want to find a connection with them, and there are some people you just don't want to find that connection with. 'So, Adolf, interesting fact: we are both vegetarians.'

I don't think that Joe Rogan is just asking questions, no. You know who I think was just asking questions? The Baha Men. They were just asking questions, and the main question they had was, 'Who let the dogs out?' As far as I know they had no agenda. They were not angry about the dogs being out.

184

They were curious. Maybe they had been at the studio all day long and were worried that the dogs had been locked inside, and when they got home they were excited to see the dogs in the backyard and they asked, 'Who let the dogs out? Hey, that is good, men, write that down.'

What I do know is that the Baha Men did not have one of the most influential podcasts in the world where they would invite someone on who had ideas about who *really* let the dogs out. If you know what I mean.

30

JULIA

I have a podcast. I think it's compulsory now for everyone to have one, but I have had one since the main question we got asked about the show was, 'What's a podcast?' When people asked me that question in the early days, I would say it was like an imaginary radio show that no-one can sack you from. Little did I know, that was a blessing and a curse.

In 2010 my friend Charlie Clausen and I started our podcast *TOFOP*. People often ask me what the show is about, and the only explanation I can give them is that the show has been around so long it's from before podcasts needed to be *about something*. It was about . . . an hour long, and even that wasn't guaranteed. If we'd known that podcasting would become a big thing, we probably would have called the show something we didn't have to constantly explain for a decade.

We jokingly describe the show as 'cool things for cool people', but when we asked our listeners once to describe what our show was, the best they could come up with was 'a comedy conversation between two old mates'. Which means either we've got to get more creative listeners or we have to do a better show, and I think it's the latter. More than anything it has been an excuse to have a weekly conversation with a friend, and for the listeners to follow that friendship through our lives. Put simply, we're here for each other's bullshit. There's been career changes and deaths to deal with, and the world has changed in so many ways since we started. In that time we've had marriages and kids, and when I say 'we', I mean Charlie. But it takes a village.

During the pandemic, our weekly conversation became a life-saver, and Charlie, myself and Podcast Mike, our producer, became a little community with our own language and in-jokes. One of which almost got way out of hand.

To understand the background of this, you need to know that I am not confident when it comes to social media and technology. I constantly feel like I am barely keeping up and will get left behind any moment now. I feel like someone in an old western running behind the train, and with any stumble I will fall over and the train will drive away and leave me behind.

When it comes to emojis, I didn't use any of them for a very long time. I didn't really understand them, and there seemed to be way too many for me to ever understand. I didn't have the brain space for that. I was too busy trying to remember internet passwords. Also, I am aware that some emojis have double meanings and I really didn't want to mislead someone I was genuinely inviting over because I was cooking eggplant.

The first emoji I ever sent was a thumbs-up. I felt like that was a pretty safe area. A yellow thumb, by the way; I know that you can apparently change them to your skin colour but in this day and age somehow changing my colour to the white one really felt like a statement I wasn't wanting to make. I don't identify as white, I identify as factory settings.

After that I branched out until I had three or four in my roster. The love heart and heart-breaking emojis seemed handy, and fingers crossed was getting some use. There's one that looks like two hands in prayer that I believe means *Thank you*. At least I hope it does. Because that is how I have been using it. No-one has said anything, so either it is *Thank you* or people think I have found religion and they are just being respectful about it.

Then there is a little yellow man with sunglasses that I believe means *Cool*. That makes sense, right? When I see someone wearing sunglasses I think that is a cool person. Or I think it is sunny. Or sometimes I think it is sunny but I can also tell that person is the type who would be wearing sunglasses whether it was sunny or not. But anyway, I think that one means *Cool* so that's how I would use it.

And I used it a lot when we were organising *TOFOP*. If someone suggested a time and I agreed, I would just send in my little *Cool* man. If someone was running late, I would send my little *Cool* man. If someone suggested a topic for the show, put on your sunglasses, little yellow man, you are going to work: *Cool*.

Then one day out of the blue, Charlie said, 'I have been meaning to ask, what does that little yellow man with sunglasses mean?'

So of course I immediately went into a panic because I assumed I was wrong, and that for months I had been sending something to people that I thought meant *Cool* but really meant something else completely. 'Ah, Wil, he has those glasses on because he is blind. You have been sending some really offensive messages. You are cancelled.'

Luckily, before I could go into too much of a spiral, Podcast Mike chipped in. 'It means *Cool*.'

This led to a discussion about what Charlie had thought it meant, which led to a discussion about how it reminded us of a picture of a former Australian prime minister wearing what can only be described as speed-dealer sunglasses. (I will give you a moment right now to google the photo: if you search for 'Tony Abbott Speed Dealer Sunnies', it will come straight up. I checked.)

It looked so right, I crudely scrawled the word 'cool' on his forehead and that became what I would send in reply to messages instead of my original yellow emoji. One day I decided I would take it to the next level. Because of the pandemic we could not record the show in person, which meant I could set the background on my video screen to whatever I wanted. I decided my background for the show would be Tony Abbott in his speed-dealer sunnies with *cool* written on his forehead. Our show would truly be cool things for cool people.

During the latest decade, Charlie and I didn't just do our *TOFOP* show, we actually had a stable of shows. One of the shows I launched in 2014 was called *Wilosophy*, where, according to the iTunes description written months before the first episode was recorded, 'Wil Anderson asks smart people stupid questions to try and work out the meaning of life. Or something.' It's not actually a bad description of what the show still is, and the smart people have included comedians, musicians, writers, sports people and even one former prime minister.

I found out during the pandemic that the former prime minister Julia Gillard was willing to be a guest on the show, and as a fellow Western Bulldogs fan I was happy to have her on. But I knew that I would have to do my research. I would read the book she had written, and most importantly I needed to make sure that when we recorded the interview I had changed the background on my screen.

I was so worried about something going wrong that the morning of the interview I logged on early with Podcast Mike, to make sure he could not see the cool background. When we were convinced it was all safe, we connected the former prime minister to the call. I can't explain what happened next, other than to guess that somehow in connecting the call my screen reset and so just as Julia was logging on, the giant Tony Abbott in speed-dealer glasses with the word *cool* on his forehead appeared behind me. I immediately knew I couldn't let the former PM see the screen, so instead I did the only thing I could think of. I slammed my laptop screen shut like a teenager who has been caught watching porn and then threw it across the room. In retrospect I admit throwing it across the room probably didn't help much.

I fetched my computer, erased the photo from it completely and then logged back on. The faces of Podcast Mike and the former prime minister Julia Gillard appeared on my screen. I said the only thing I could think of. 'Sorry, I don't know what happened. The internet dropped out. I live near Mullumbimby, somebody probably burned down the 5G tower.'

31

TIMELINE

I tried not to live in fear of Covid, but the truth is I was afraid of it. I still am. It's hard to believe there was a time I wasn't, but a man who I patted on the head will beg to differ. But early on I was less afraid of catching the virus, I was more afraid of appearing in the newspaper with a Covid timeline. One of the things I know about the media is that once you have a timeline you are in trouble, and at the start of the pandemic the media loved a timeline.

I am glad we have moved on from the public shaming that was so common at the start. Every time there was a case identified in the community, the newspapers would print a timeline of everything that person had done in the previous few days. I understand that people were afraid of the virus, but I lived in fear of that timeline. It felt so unfair. It was not their fault they had caught a virus we now know can get to anyone no matter how careful they are, and while they were worried about possibly dying from a deadly virus no-one knew much about, they were at the same time dealing with everyone else judging their life choices.

And judge we did. Their life was on display for judgement. 'This guy checks out too many barbecues—just buy a barbecue and go home, mate!'

We don't really do that for other diseases. 'This man has skin cancer. Well, let's publish a timeline of where he has been. Has he been out in the sun? With his complexion? Did he Slip, Slop, Slap? Did he wear a wide-brimmed hat or just a cap? Why are his ears so weird? And did you see this receipt? Apparently he bought a giant tub of Vaseline and a roast chicken. What a pervert!'

I don't think any of us would really like our whole lives taken out of context for public inspection. I have stuff to hide. We all have stuff to hide. So for a while I lived my life purely based on how it would look in the newspaper. I tried not to do anything embarrassing, but if I did I immediately went into self-imposed lockdown. 'Sorry, I can't go out for a couple of days, I did something really stupid this morning and I don't want to read about it in the paper.'

I wasn't too worried because I followed the rules, but like most people I had the rare occasion when for whatever reason I thought the rules did not apply to me. One of those was the first time I was tested for Covid. The Northern Rivers was free of Covid and people were living their lives in pretty normal fashion, but I had to go to the city for work and do a Covid test before I travelled.

I went to the local hospital where the testing centre had been set up and I was the only one there. In fact, I think the staff were pretty happy to see me. I don't think they had too many visitors in the early days and they were grateful for the practice run. Despite my being the only person there, they ran through the whole procedure, moving from station to station and stop to stop. I felt like I was on a military parade for the Queen.

When I arrived at the final station, I had essentially just done a lap of an empty office space, and was greeted by the doctor wielding a cotton bud. She had obviously been rehearsing for this moment. 'Now, I need to warn you, this is going to tickle a little.' And then she asked something I hadn't expected. 'Have you ever had wasabi?'

I nodded my head. I didn't think this was the time to mention I had once eaten sushi with my cat. She said, 'Well, it's just going to feel like you have had too much wasabi.'

I told her I appreciated the warning, but as a professional stand-up comedian of 25-plus years I could guarantee her I had had worse things up my nose. In fact, you can put anything up there as long as it isn't pollen, because if I get any of that in there my immune system thinks trees are trying to murder me.

After I had the test, they told me that technically under the rules I now had to go home and isolate until I got the result. This was one of those moments when you understand why the rule exists: if there is any suspicion you have something, then you should isolate so you don't spread it. But that was not me. I was just doing the right thing for work. If I hadn't had the test I would have been free to move around the community, so I didn't think I should be penalised just because I was doing the right thing.

In the end, I compromised. I decided I would only do the things that were absolutely necessary and then stay home for the rest of it. Unfortunately, one of the things I did have to do was go to an open house for a real estate inspection. I had some friends who were looking to move to an area near where we lived, but they were currently in lockdown in another city. So I needed to go and check out the house for them. Always good to send the eagle eye of a man who can't identify a wood pile on his own property.

Real details man, me.

But I convinced myself it was the right thing to do because I was doing something nice for my friends, and I was masked and incredibly careful. I really couldn't concentrate on checking out the house properly, because the whole time I was thinking, 'This would look terrible on a timeline. A real estate open home? Who do you think you are—Dave Hughes?'

For two years I postponed more shows than I performed. It had been months since I had been on stage, but there were two shows in my calendar that hadn't been cancelled. Well, that wasn't entirely true; scheduled in 2020, they were postponed to 2021, and looked like they were going to finally go ahead.

The shows were in Wagga Wagga at the Wagga Wagga Comedy Festival. For those who don't know, the previous time I had visited the Wagga Wagga Comedy Festival had not ended well. I was wrongfully arrested on the flight, taken to the police station, almost missed my show, got cleared of it all and ended up writing an entire show about it called *WILEGAL* that I had toured all over Australia. The one place I hadn't taken the show was Wagga Wagga.

It had been a couple of years since the incident had happened, a couple of years of getting social media messages from people with pictures of them inside the Wagga Wagga airport asking, 'Does this remind you of something?' The funny thing is, it doesn't. It doesn't remind me of anything because I didn't make it inside the airport. They took me straight to the police station from the tarmac, so the joke's on them.

I thought it was time to take the show to Wagga Wagga. The final line of *WILEGAL* was actually the first line I had improvised on stage the night I was arrested. 'So, a funny thing happened on the way to the show.' It felt like full circle.

It's one thing to tell the story, another to tell it in front of the people who were there that night—people who are featured in the story. Is the way I remember it the way *they* remember it? Of course, many of the people in the show had already seen it, including the police. In fact, one of the police involved came to see the show and sent me a message that simply said, 'Let me know if you need another lift from the airport.'

That did raise a big question: How was I going to get there? My immediate thought was that I couldn't fly. I just didn't feel ready to risk a sequel, but more importantly I was worried about Covid and flying didn't feel safe at the time. I know airlines make you wear a mask. But they do let you take it off for meals. I am no scientist but I suspect that method doesn't fool Covid. It would be great if it turned out that you couldn't catch Covid when you were eating and drinking, but if that were true then there wouldn't have been so many cases in America.

So anyway, I decided I would drive. I knew that the drive was possible; that's how I had got back home from Wagga Wagga last time. Actually I decided I would drive to Sydney myself, and then get a driver to take me the rest of the way. I almost considered hiring a limo so I could roll into town standing up with my head out the sunroof. It would be good for my back and Covid-safe.

I had two shows booked Saturday and Sunday night and they were both sold out. Turns out if you want to move a lot of tickets in a town, have an incident there and then write a whole show about it. It would have been a better career move to get arrested on a flight to New York, but probably a lot more scary.

I decided I would drive out my winding road on the Friday and down to Sydney. Then I could get up Saturday morning and get driven to Wagga for the show. I packed some food so I wouldn't have to stop anywhere along the way, and made it to Sydney. When I woke up on Saturday morning I realised I had no milk, so I thought I would go out for a walk and a coffee. That was allowed under the rules and I thought it was pretty low risk. There were no Sydney cases at the time.

There were three places to grab a coffee at the local village shops, but in my opinion there was one clear standout. When I got close I realised the place I wanted to go to had a long line and I considered going to one of the other places, but instead did another lap of the block and waited for the line to get shorter. Coffee in hand, I headed home, got picked up and headed to Wagga Wagga.

I was pretty nervous about the show that night, but I shouldn't have been. It was amazing, it felt part comedy show and part reunion, so I went home to my Wagga Wagga motel feeling satisfied. It felt like a chapter in my life was coming to a close.

The next morning I woke up early and felt like a coffee. I didn't know where the best coffee in Wagga Wagga was, but I decided that would be my mission for the morning. I got a little medicated so that my hips wouldn't hurt while I was walking around, and I walked the streets of Wagga Wagga drinking coffee and eating snacks. It felt peaceful. My last visit had been so horrible; this felt healing.

The show that night was also fun, and immediately afterwards I was driven back to Sydney. The next morning I woke up early, got in the car and drove home.

I was feeling pretty proud of what I had achieved, when I woke up the next day and saw the news that there was a new Covid infection in the community, a case that ended up sparking a huge spike in Sydney and shutting down the city. The poor man who had a timeline was dubbed the Sydney Limo Driver, and on his timeline for Saturday morning was a stop at my local shops for a coffee.

Shit. Shit. Shit. Shit. He had coffee at the same village, in vaguely the same time period. The only good news was that he hadn't gone to the exact same cafe, but to the one a few doors down with the shorter line. I was still panicking. What if I brushed by him or something? What if I had Covid, and even worse, what if I took it to Wagga Wagga? I was going to get permanently banned from that city. *What do you have against us?*

Also, I knew my timeline would not look great. I had performed to 1000 unmasked people and then walked the streets of Wagga Wagga all day long. It would have looked like I was *trying* to spread it around. *Why did he have so many cups of coffee? And also, why did he go to that Muffin Break not once but twice? I bet he just ate the tops off the muffins and threw the rest away and then went back and bought some more muffins and ate the tops off them too.* I don't want people making assumptions like that about me, especially when they are right.

I didn't end up having Covid. It turned out that the limo driver actually stopped for his slightly inferior coffee an hour after I had picked up mine. But it did make me think how amazing it was that the Australian government spent $9 million on a Covid Safe app that didn't find one case, but I nearly tripped over one on the way to the shops.

32

BANANAS

People judge those who believe in conspiracy theories harshly, but I have some empathy for them. I like to walk a mile in their shoes, even if sometimes they aren't wearing any shoes. I get it. There is a part of us as humans that just wants to feel like there is an explanation for stuff, no matter how weird that explanation might sound. After all, that's what religions are, right? They are just conspiracy theories that have been around for long enough that people tend to pay them more respect. Also, I know there will be some people who are mad at this comparison. 'Come on, Wil, my faith is completely different from something ridiculous like QAnon. I mean, they believe that they are getting secret commandments from an anonymous source that they have to follow, and they believe that JFK Junior is going to rise from the dead, whereas I believe that . . . Well, I believe I have picked some bad examples. Happy Easter.'

I think the hardest thing to accept in life is the idea that there is no grand plan. That there is no magic man in the sky or consortium of lizard people who are running everything. For some people that is too much; they want to believe that no matter how fucked up things are it's because someone somewhere has a plan. Even if that plan is horrible and cruel and doesn't really make any sense if you think about it for more than a second.

And I get it. I get the appeal of feeling like you are in on a secret, that you have some special knowledge that makes you smarter than the average person. Sure, to the average person your ideas probably make you seem like a complete idiot, but that's just because they haven't woken up yet. They are still a sheep, *baaaaa*.

The other reason people believe in conspiracies is that sometimes they are just fun. I was watching some footage from an American rally, I think it was for QAnon, one of those events that starts with a march and has the potential to end in some *storming*.

There was this lovely kind-looking lady, dressed head-to-toe in garments that seemed to be exclusively made out of the American flag. She was being interviewed and started the conversation by saying, 'I know this sounds bananas!'

She immediately had my attention, because in my experience these people usually believe that what they are saying makes complete sense. In fact, you can usually tell how full of shit someone is by how many times they tell you it is common sense.

This woman being interviewed said, 'I know this sounds bananas!' And I leaned in and turned up the television. If even *she* thought it sounded bananas, then time for me to get in my pyjamas and start coming down the stairs. I lost control of that sentence there a bit. She said, 'I know this sounds bananas, but the other night at a Rolling Stones concert . . .' Every second it was getting more interesting, and I was getting more interested. She said, 'I know this sounds bananas, but the other night at a Rolling Stones concert . . . Prince came back from the dead.'

I need to pause here for a moment, because her explanation of this conspiracy is not over yet, but I don't want to rush through the details. So far, we have a Rolling Stones concert and Prince coming back to life. Sure, why not? If any human looked like he had the power to transcend death and return from the other side, Prince is as good a nomination as any. And why wouldn't he want to come back to Earth and go to a gig? Maybe his last regret was that he never got to see the Stones.

If she had stopped telling her story there, I would have been satisfied. But she continued, 'I know this sounds bananas, but the other night at a Rolling Stones concert Prince came back from the dead and entered the body of Keith Richards.'

This was amazing. She was saying that there was a Rolling Stones gig and in the middle of it Prince rose from the dead and entered the body of Keith Richards. I guess it isn't the worst thing he has had in his body. She was right: Get Gwen

Stefani, because this shit is bananas and we need someone to spell it out. At this point even the Big Banana at Coffs Harbour was thinking: 'This is too bananas for me.'

But she was still not done. She said, 'I know this sounds bananas, but the other night at a Rolling Stones concert Prince came back from the dead and entered the body of Keith Richards . . . and then Michael Jackson came back from the dead and entered the body of Mick Jagger and he even moonwalked. There is evidence of it. It is true.'

Now I knew she had gone too far. I was willing to believe that Prince would come back and combine with Keith to create the greatest guitarist of all time, but there was no way known that Michael Jackson would enter the body of an age-appropriate man. I shall now pause for people to put down their books and applaud that joke.

I get why people believe conspiracy theories. It's good to be sceptical about what you read and watch. You can't trust everyone in the media, and I know that because I am in the media and I don't trust myself. You should be sceptical of the media or the 'Tell Lies Vision', as one of my neighbours is fond of calling it.

But not all conspiracy theories are fun like this one. Sometimes they get very dark, very quickly. For example, it is good not to trust the claims of politicians. Sometimes they do lie, sometimes they are just incompetent, but it is a leap from that to accusing those politicians of storing children in tunnels under the city, which was one of the accusations made during the pandemic. Politicians are not storing kids in tunnels under the city, although during lockdown I knew people who would have gladly shoved their kids down a manhole if it gave them a few hours of peace. 'Get down there, I will throw your books down there with you, this is where you are home-schooling now.'

It's the same with the people who claim the world is run by shapeshifting lizards. That seems harmless enough until you realise that when they say 'lizards', they don't generally mean literal lizards. They distract you with the shapeshifting lizard chat and while you are not paying attention they come in quickly with the terms and conditions. 'We believe the world is run by shapeshifting lizards, and also the Holocaust never happened.'

Hang on, what now? We were having a nice chat about lizards and then you made it weird. Yes, it turns out that when they talk about lizards running everything they are talking about the lizards from *Schindler's Lizards*. (I should point out that I do not believe the world is run by shapeshifting lizards, but even if it is, shush it and don't make a fuss. I mean, what are we going to do about it? We are never going to be able to track them down; they are shapeshifters.)

When someone tells me there is a secret cabal running everything, all I can ever think is, 'You have clearly never organised a surprise party of any kind.' If the lizards have managed to run things in secret for so long without most people finding out, then I say let them keep running things.

A lot of conspiracy theories used to feel harmless and fun, but things have changed for the worse. We now see rallies where yoga instructors and wellness types are marching alongside neo-Nazis. How did we screw things up so badly that those two are hanging out together? You know something is wrong with the world when a Nazi is throwing their arm in the air and the yoga instructor is saying, 'You know, to get the full stretch you really want to breathe the whole way through the *Sieg Heil*.' The world is fucked up when wellness types are befriending Nazis. I think you misheard when you thought he said he wanted to go on a *juice cleanse*.

People believe lots of stupid things, but at the moment we live in a world where people have been lost down some rabbit holes and if we are going to face the challenges in front of us we need to get them back.

I used to believe that one of the best ways to defeat misinformation was with facts, but if the last few years have taught me anything it's that if facts didn't get someone into something in the first place, facts aren't the thing that is going to get them back out again. That is like trying to lure Hansel and Gretel away from the cake house and out of the forest by leaving a trail of carrots and celery sticks.

Facts didn't get them in, so facts aren't going to get them out. I had this argument with a friend of mine who was adamant. 'No, Wil, the way to get people to change their mind is to show them more facts and better facts.' To which I showed them several links to reputable peer-reviewed studies that showed that is not the case; in fact, the opposite can be true and it can just make them double down on their false narrative. After reading the links I had sent them, they just replied, 'Well, you haven't changed my mind.' And I thought that probably proved the point I was trying to make.

We need to pull these people out of their rabbit holes, away from fighting imaginary enemies and back to the Christmas table. Because that's the harsh reality of what has happened. Conspiracies aren't a bit of fun anymore; they are tearing apart families, friends and communities.

I think one of the major things that will stop people coming back from these fringe groups is that they know we will bring it up. They would love to be able to come back and join the family for Dad's birthday, but they know that someone is going to mention that during the pandemic they joined QAnon and wrote to the Vatican asking for their real birth certificate and umbilical cord back. That was a real thing that people did, by the way, which must have been a surprise to the Pope when he was going through his mail. I hope he put one of the cardinals on it and made them write back to each one, like the people who answer a kid's letter to Santa. (Side note: I hope if you are writing to the Vatican asking for your umbilical cord back, then you at least have the courtesy to include a stamped self-addressed envelope for the return.)

They are not going to come back to Christmas if we keep bringing these sorts of things up, so we have to promise not to, and that is why I propose a Covid bad-decisions amnesty. I think everyone should be able to nominate a couple of bad decisions they made during the pandemic, hand them back in and no-one can ever bring them up again. You joined QAnon, I watched *Tiger King*; they were both mistakes. I encouraged other people to watch it, I told them it was good. It was not good. I was wrong, let's never mention it again. You wrote to the Vatican for your umbilical cord, I bought a vat of Vaseline and a roast chicken; we never need to talk about either of those things again. You marched alongside a neo-Nazi at a rally, I bought a really expensive exercise bike, because I was going to get fit while I couldn't travel and it would be really good for strengthening my hips. The only exercise I got was lugging it down to where my fake comedy club used to be and letting it sit there untouched for eighteen months. Then at the end of 2021, I looked at that bike and said to myself, 'Ando, 2022 is going to be the year of the exercise bike.' Then, mistakenly on a couple of levels, I watched the reboot of *Sex and the City* and in the first episode the character Big died on that exact same expensive exercise bike and *just like that* it was hard rubbish. Anyway, what I am saying is, we all did some dumb things, so can we leave it at that and move on?

We need these people back because we have real problems facing us as a species and we could actually use their skills. You want to uncover a conspiracy by a group that is secretly controlling our society from the shadows by using their immense wealth to pay off politicians and control the media? A group that is destroying the world for all of humanity simply so they can profit? You don't need to invent an enemy, there already is one. They are called the fossil fuel companies.

The fossil fuel companies knew about the effects they were having on the climate before anyone else did, and then actively covered it up so they could make more money. You don't need to make up evidence of this; they've admitted it. They continually commissioned and buried reports, and luckily for them they had plenty of holes they were digging in the earth in which to bury them.

You can use your skills to do some research, and the good news is that a bunch of scientists have done a bunch of peer-reviewed reports so it will be easy to catch up. The IPCC puts out so many reports about the effects of climate change that they are now a major contributor to deforestation.

Wait until you find out how little tax the fossil fuel companies have paid, how many incentives they have taken, all while destroying the planet for profit. You need a Big Bad? Here you go. The IPCC said human activity was the unequivocal cause of the climate emergency. The fossil fuel industry replied, 'We would like a second opinion . . . And we are going to trust this one more because we paid for it.'

The fossil fuel companies knew they were destroying the Earth and they kept doing it. You'd think if you knew your product was killing people and you covered it up to make more cash you would end up in prison, but instead it's been a case of, 'Well, that is very naughty . . . Would you like some tax concessions?'

Some might argue, 'Well, you would protect your industry in the same situation.' But I know that is not true. At the start of the pandemic, when there was a risk that comedy could spread Covid, we stopped doing comedy. We recognised that comedy was a super-spreader: you are gathering people in poorly ventilated rooms to get them to expel fluids from their mouths as often as possible, and the funnier you are the more deadly. So we stopped. We shut an entire industry down to help others. We didn't employ some lobbyists to cover it up. We didn't come up with some bullshit pledge to transition to clean comedy (although doing clean comedy would probably result in fewer laughs and in turn make it less risky). Clean comedy during a pandemic would not be jokes without swearing, it would be jokes without punchlines.

We didn't try to claim that we weren't responsible and mount bullshit arguments in our defence, like, 'Come on, forget vaccines, laughter is the best medicine.' All I am saying is there is something wrong when the clowns have higher standards than the fossil fuel companies.

Of course there are climate change sceptics too, and I hope they are right. Let me be clear: the majority of scientists don't think they are right, but I hope they are. If the scientists are right, then we are in a lot of trouble and we are not doing anywhere near enough about it. This is one time I want to trust a dickhead over an expert.

I shouldn't call them sceptics, by the way; they are deniers. A sceptic is someone who weighs the available evidence and finds the current interpretation of that evidence to be flawed in some way. But these people are deniers; they read two Andrew Bolt articles and had their opinions peer-reviewed by their cat.

They are the sort of people whose arguments run along the lines of, 'It's cold outside—what happened to your global warming?' Forget warming, I have a warning. If you are about to bring up that fucking poem I am going to go bananas. 'It's cold, what happened to global warming?' is an argument that makes as much sense as saying it's dark outside, what happened to the sun? How are your fancy solar panels going to work now that there is no sun?

But I still hope they are right. Again, I should point out that they are almost certainly not right, but I really hope they are. That is the best-case scenario, that this has all been a giant con perpetrated by the climate scientists of the world for some reason that can never be fully explained and that the climate is not changing in a way that will end lives, ruin habitats and lead to the extinction of species, maybe even our own. I have really got my fingers crossed that the dickheads have fluked this one.

I hope they are right (note: They are not). I don't care if I am right, I am not qualified to have an opinion. I trust the scientists are probably right, and that terrifies me. I don't want them to be right, I don't want to be right, I just don't want to be under water. I am happy to have egg on my face as long as the egg isn't being fried by the extreme heat we are living in.

I hope the dickheads are right and the scientists are wrong, but I don't think that is the case. The scientists get accused of being alarmist. They are not alarmist, they are just alarmed. It is okay to yell 'Fire!' in a crowded theatre if the theatre is actually on fire. That is like the guard at the bank saying, 'Yes, I did let the people come in with stockings on their heads and holding guns . . . but I didn't want to alarm anyone!' Scientists are not alarmist. They can hear the alarm going off and they are trying to warn us. We are pretending that we can't hear the alarm. We are making excuses in our heads not to do anything yet. We are pushing snooze on Doomsday. 'Can't we have just another ten years? I will get there by 2050 at the latest.'

The truth is that, rather than being too alarmist, sometimes scientists aren't alarmist enough. That's because they know that a feeling of complete helplessness can lead to inaction. If we think things are too bad, then we might be like, 'Fuck it. The planet is ruined anyway, I might as well spray this deodorant into the air and burn this huge pile of tyres I have in the backyard.'

Although on the flip side it can take the pressure off your day-to-day. 'Oops, I didn't remember to pick up the milk, but the Earth is facing a total extinction of life so I guess that puts it in perspective. I didn't clean the fridge, but the oil and coal companies didn't clean up their mess either so I shouldn't feel too guilty.' That's a real glass-half-empty meets glass-half-full approach.

The scientists are trying their best, but we have to be honest: another report is not going to change anything. Anyone who *can* be convinced by a report *has* been convinced by a report. Every time a report comes out, things are just worse. The only thing that has changed now is that we have fewer trees. The next time they put out a report it should be two words: 'Still Fucked.'

That's why I have got to hope the scientists are wrong and the dickheads are right this time. Even the Washington Generals beat the Harlem Globetrotters once. Maybe this is the one time. Maybe the deniers are right, that the climate scientists have just been in it for the money. I have actually heard people make that argument: 'You know they are just worried about their funding drying up!' No, they are worried about our clean water supplies drying up! That is the bigger issue.

I love the idea that there are a bunch of scientists who thought, 'Well, I could go and work for one of these massive oil and gas companies making billions from slowing down clean energy and help them produce reports covering it up, but I want some of that sweet climate change cash.'

Yes, we all know the richest people in our society are climate scientists. They are always strutting around in their mink lab coats, using Bunsen burners to light expensive cigars.

'We can't make it rain in drought areas, but I can make it rain in the strip club later! It's getting hot in here, so take off all your clothes; it's hot because of increased methane in the air!'

33

DELAY

I once got sacked from a job on commercial radio but they allowed us to run out the remaining six weeks on our contract. That was brave of them. Those six weeks on air were some of the most fun entertainment I have ever made. We had nothing to lose so we tried out every dumb idea we had. It was like a going-out-of-business sale for ideas that we had hoped would sustain many more years. Everything had to go. When one newspaper column highlighted how much we were doing and commented that some radio shows started to phone it in when they were not being renewed, we thought that was a great idea and phoned in an entire show. Literally phoned it in. I was on the phone wandering the streets of Brisbane and the other host, Lehmo, had his feet in the water at Bondi Beach. We still asked the guests to go into the studio so we were the only ones on the phone.

We also stole a lot. Well, I did anyway. I stole stationery. One of the best things about working an office job, which is not something I have done much in my life, was unlimited access to the stationery cupboard. In those last six weeks I cleaned the place out. At the start I was subtle, taking a few things at a time and then shaking them out of the leg of my pants at the end of the day like I was in a prison, but by the end I was just carrying armfuls of it out brazenly past the boss's desk. I think my back-up plan was that if I didn't land another job, I could at least start an Officeworks.

Anyway, the point I am trying to make is the fossil fuel companies know they are being sacked soon, and the planet is their stationery cupboard. They are going to steal as much as they can until their office security passes don't work anymore.

Climate-change denial has become climate delay. It's just a plan to buy some more time to steal A4 and highlighters. Our country is one of the most susceptible to climate change, but also one of the slowest to do anything about it, because for years we have been digging valuable things out of the earth and selling them to countries overseas. Australia has been like a giant Kinder Surprise; when they cracked that layer they found a toy inside. Which is not a bad analogy if the toy in a Kinder Surprise was also responsible for warming the planet and killing millions of people.

It's no accident that the plans for future soft climate targets have been endorsed by the same people and media that used to peddle climate-change denial. Delay is the new denial. More time to clean out the stationery cupboard. The idea of 2050 targets is the most damaging because it makes us feel like we are doing something when mostly what we are doing is promising to do something by 2050. We live in an Afterpay world, and this is an Afterpay solution. Net zero means a pledge to take as much carbon out of the atmosphere by 2050 as we put in. It's a real hokey-pokey plan. The major problem is we are doing a lot of the hokey at the moment and not much of the pokey. We are not driving a winding road, but we are doing something even more dangerous. We are speeding towards a wall, and instead of pumping the brakes, we are putting the foot down on the accelerator and hoping someone invents some magic brakes before we crash. It's a plan that seems to be based on Cameron's plan to wind back the odometer on his dad's car in *Ferris Bueller's Day Off*, so that should work fine.

To put it another way, what we are currently doing is like if I pledged to give up smoking pot by 2050 but instead of starting to slow down now, I actually smoked some more pot for a while (well, I couldn't spring that on the weed-related industries I support; won't someone think of the bong makers and Uber Eats?) but pledged by 2050 to come up with a machine that would suck the smoke back out of my lungs. The good news is that if I don't make it, I will just pay some people in some other countries to stop smoking pot on my behalf and claim that as credits.

At the moment our approach is like someone saying, 'We are going to have to make some plans to get this guy to the hospital and get some medical attention for all his injuries!' That is very considerate and compassionate of you, but you are also the person who is hitting him. Do you think you could just stop hitting him? Or at the very least, don't hit him so hard? And now you have started kicking him. You definitely don't need to do that. What do you have to say for yourself? 'Yeah, he is in real trouble. He is going to have so many issues. We need to put a lot into funding this hospital because he is going to have a range of injuries and ailments that will need treating.'

Australia has been the drug dealer, growing rich on something that is fucking up the planet. 'Come on, guys, try some coal. Don't be afraid of it. All the cool kids are doing it. Coal sounds a lot like cool!' You know what won't be cool? Global temperatures. We have justified it on the grounds of people needing our resources for good reasons, but we think we are Walter White when we are really Heisenberg. We have been selling our sweet brown meth to the world. And now the planet is breaking, bad.

We have been convinced by the fossil fuel companies' expensive PR that climate solutions are in our individual hands, when about 100 corporations are responsible for over 70 percent of emissions. That's like your boss coming around for dinner, doing a shit in the middle of the table, making you all eat it and then blaming the smell on the dog farting. Sure, recycling and composting don't hurt, but they don't really help that much either. It's a magic trick: 'If we can convince them that they can solve climate change by remembering their Keep Cup, then that might keep them from seizing the state. They certainly can't decarbonise the economy without their morning coffee.'

When it comes to climate change, the greatest trick the fossil fuel companies ever played was convincing us that it's like every jacket I owned in the eighties: reversible. That somehow, if we just hit a few targets, we will be able to turn the thermostat on the world back a few degrees. That will be great, won't it? And even better, all the extinct species will come back to life as well; it will be some real Thanos meets Dr Dolittle shit.

34

CHANGE

Part of the problem with how we deal with climate change is how we talk about it. Even the term itself: climate change. 'Change' sounds like it could be a good thing: a change of outfit, some loose change, a change is as good as a holiday. We are not dealing with climate change, we are dealing with a climate emergency. And no-one has ever said a change is as good as an emergency. We need to do something now. You can't spell emergency without urgency. (Well, actually you can, and do, but that seems like a real missed opportunity to me.)

The media have a huge role to play. If the biggest issues facing humanity could be ranked for gravity, the climate emergency would be the lead story every night. Instead, for too long the media indulged in false balance when it came to the climate debate. 'We have a climate scientist on to talk about global warming, so for balance we should also get Uncle Dave who can't reverse park because he thinks the Earth is flat. He has Google Maps and a copy of a poem that he thinks refutes it all.'

Even the weather reports tend to describe extreme weather in sensationalist ways. They talk about 'record-breaking' heatwaves. I am fine with things being described as record-breaking when we are talking about the Olympics, or you've got the guys from *Guinness* around and you've shoved 150 golf balls in your mouth. But when it comes to weather, they are more record-melting heatwaves, as in it is hot enough that your record collection will melt. 'Shit, my copy of "Ice Ice Baby" is now "Warm Puddle Baby"!'

I was watching the weather report one night, and in the same segment they mentioned it was the hottest it had ever been in Sydney, while in Canberra it was snowing. Goulburn, in between the two, was hot but hailing the size of cricket balls. Half of South Australia was on fire and Brisbane was flooding. They continued with the segment as usual. I would not have been able to do that. I would have stopped right there and turned to the camera and started yelling, 'What the fuck is going on? Hey, Australia, I think there might be something wrong when the weather report is: "Today's weather, *all* of it. We recommend you take an umbrella, a fire extinguisher and a cricket bat."'

The media can play a powerful role in raising awareness of these issues, changing people's minds, getting them to act. I remember one afternoon in the Before Times when some people came over for a Sunday afternoon barbecue. It got towards the evening and there were a few stragglers lingering, pondering whether to pack up or kick on as the sun went down, but the thing I love about having people over to my house is that when I want to go home, I am already there. I can leave the party without technically *leaving*. All I need to do is go into the other room. I decided to go inside, take a little medicine and watch a documentary. By the way, that is the real definition of middle age: when you leave a party to watch a documentary.

I turned my TV to the ABC, and by that I mean I turned on my TV and it was on the ABC because I only watch the ABC and never watch any other network. Why would I? The ABC is the best and I am not being paid to say this. I am definitely saying this of my own free will, and I am not being threatened. I most certainly have not had a call from ABC management telling me they already have the hole they can bury me in if I do the wrong thing.

On the ABC was a documentary about the Great Barrier Reef presented by Sir David Attenborough and, spoilers, it turns out the Great Barrier Reef is in danger of becoming the Not-So-Great Barrier Reef and then the Fine Barrier Reef if we don't do something soon. The documentary was captivating as Sir Dave explored this stunning underwater universe. This might seem like the dumbest statement of all, and I have said some dumb things, but I remember thinking, I didn't know the Great Barrier Reef was *this* great.

As inspiring as the world he was introducing me to was the man doing the introductions. Sir David Attenborough was nearly 90 when he made this documentary series. There was one scene where they only had a half-hour window to film on a particular reef before the tide rose and covered it and Sir David managed to land there, film the segment and get back out, all in his late eighties. I couldn't believe that was really his age, until I looked down at the footwear he was wearing as he shot his links on the reef and I spotted a pair of Crocs. Okay, yes, he is almost 90.

It wasn't just standing above the reef where Sir David did his work. There is a scene where he pilots a submersible called the Triton deeper on the reef than anyone had ever been before. Isn't that incredible? At his age, to be exploring a part of the world where no-one had ever been. To be fair, he hadn't intended to end up all the way down there, but he took a wrong turn. He also had the indicator on the whole way, and was trying to tune in the AM radio. These are jokes about old people and driving, and are completely disrespectful to a legend like Sir David. I really should not try to be funny all the time.

At the end of this series, Sir David Attenborough breaks the rule of a lifetime and decides to editorialise. He stares at the camera after being our tour guide through what I am now lobbying to be renamed the Fucking Great Barrier Reef, and asks a question. 'Do we really care so little about the Earth on which we live that we don't want to protect one of the greatest wonders from the consequences of our behaviour?'

I am sure he was only saying it because his parents told him to, but despite that I started crying. Crying like I had never cried before. Crying for the reef, crying for the planet, crying for Sir David.

It was at this moment that everyone who was in the back-yard decided to wrap up the party and come inside. The only problem was, they didn't know why I was crying. I was fine two hours earlier when I left the party, but now they had walked in on me having a breakdown on the couch. Someone asked what was wrong, and I was about to answer when another person chipped in, 'Don't worry, he's probably just been watching *The Mighty Ducks*.'

35

SPACE

I try not to judge people too harshly for believing things that aren't true, because we all believe things that aren't true. Maybe you are reading this, thinking, 'I don't believe anything that isn't true.' If that's the case, you just proved my point. You believing that you don't believe anything that isn't true is the thing you believe that isn't true. Right? Exactly. This is a nice kitchen, by the way.

We all believe things that can't be proved, and we all believe stupid things. Everyone has at least one stupid thing that they believe. It can be big or small but you have one. Believing stupid things is one of the building blocks of our society. We didn't build this city on rock and roll, we built it on believing stupid things.

Despite what we might like to think, we can all get conned into believing something that isn't true. Otherwise there would be no such thing as cryptocurrency. And I know there will be some crypto true believers reading this who will think I am wrong about that, and will want to convince me otherwise. All I would say is that you have the right to believe whatever you want to believe as long as it doesn't hurt anyone else, but don't try and convince me. Don't hit me up and try to talk me into crypto, because I have heard all the arguments and they can be summarised as 'Crypto, crypto, future, future, buy low, sell high, blockchain, buy the dip, buy the dip!' Thanks, *great chat*.

To be fair, I am paraphrasing, but not that much. We like to think that we make our judgements by considering the facts, but our brains are lawyers, not scientists, and I am the first to admit that most of the opinions I have about cryptocurrency are based on the kind of people who are really into it.

'But you don't get it, Wil. It is the future of money, it will revolutionise the entire financial system.' Yeah, maybe. Or maybe the rich will get richer and, as always, the poor will get the picture (of the worthless cartoon ape). It's the fervour of crypto fans that scares me the most; they think they have cracked the code when in most cases they have just cracked and bought some code.

I think the main reason I would never get into cryptocurrency is that I don't want to become one of those people who talk about nothing but cryptocurrency. Sure, you could just quietly buy some and keep it to yourself. I mean, I am sure you *could* do that. Just because no-one in history ever has doesn't mean it can't be done.

There is a simple reason that when you buy crypto you want to get other people into it too: it's because that's the only way it has any value. Crypto is like Santa Claus: it only has power if people believe in it. Crypto is nothing. The reason it has value is that someone has convinced you that your *nothing* is worth *something*—and it can be worth something, if you can convince someone else your nothing is worth something to them. The price of your nothing is entirely dependent on what someone else is willing to pay for it, and the world makes complete sense; everything is fine and nothing could possibly go wrong.

I had one friend say to me, 'No, Wil, you don't understand, the current financial system is completely corrupt and entrenches power and inequality.' Yes, I agree with that. I agree that you have identified the problem, I just don't think you have found the solution. 'But Wil, I am just trying to get my finances in shape!' Yes, and I can see what shape: a *pyramid*. 'No, Wil, it's not a pyramid scheme, and here is an extensive video from an expert, Professor Ponzi, to explain why.'

For the record, it is unfair to call cryptocurrency a pyramid scheme or a Ponzi scheme when it is so much more than that. Some of it is money laundering. It can also be old-fashioned artisanal standard-issue fraud. Some of it is a pump-and-dump scheme. By the way, I don't really know what a pump-and-dump scheme is, but it is fun to say. Sounds like a wank and a shit. Which reminds me of the blokes who talk to me about crypto. The point is I am not qualified to know exactly how you are being ripped off, but when people are paying a quarter of a million dollars for a cartoon picture of an ape then your Ponzi has jumped the shark. And you can buy the electronic image of that shark for $500,000.

I think my major problem with cryptocurrency is that we already have so many problems in the world, we didn't need to invent a new one. 'Hey Wil, how did you spend the last days of civilisation? Were you fighting for those less fortunate than you, lobbying on behalf of the planet, trying to end world hunger or running an election campaign for Shaun Micallef?' Well, I would have loved to be doing those things, but unfortunately I was too busy betting on the value of imaginary coins. Time and money well spent.

I know if I ever dabbled in cryptocurrency I would definitely get ripped off. There seem to be a lot of criminals involved in crypto, which is a real surprise for a currency that was originally used mostly to buy drugs and guns on the dark web. I actually know someone who used cryptocurrency to buy drugs on the dark web, and then when the value spiked he was suddenly rich from his leftover drug money, so that seems like a good basis for a safe and trustworthy financial system. But even if it hadn't started in the underworld, there would still be criminals there, because anywhere there is the promise of easy money there are suckers, and any place there are suckers there are people offering them something to suck. Gross.

I know I would get ripped off, but in a way, that wouldn't even be my biggest fear. My fear would be that I would make some stupid decision and then regret it forever. There was a guy who in 2010 bought two Papa John's pizzas using bitcoin that was worth about $40 at the time but would be worth $400 million today. I remember reading that and thinking, that would definitely be me. 'Dammit, and the pizza wasn't even that good. See, I knew there was a downside to this medicinal cannabis.'

Before the pandemic there was one person in the world worth more than $100 billion, and as I am writing there are nine. By the time you read this, that statistic will most likely be out of date. This might be controversial to some people, but I don't think *anyone* should have $100 billion. I think if you make it to $1 billion they should give you a little trophy and say, 'Congratulations, I hope you proved whatever you were trying to prove to your dad or whoever, but we are taking the rest of your money and using it to help people.' We shouldn't be celebrating people having $100 billion. That is almost enough dollars to give one to every single person who has ever lived. Although some of them would be hard to track down to dole out the money. Probably better to just split it between the people who are alive and need it. That's a much better plan, now that I think about it.

Imagine having the money to help fix climate change and not doing it. Imagine having enough money to end world hunger and not doing it. That is what a status symbol should look like. What's that, you have a room filled with classic sneakers? An airline hangar filled with vintage cars? Who gives a fuck? Good for you. This guy filled all the starving stomachs in the world for five years, so I'm more impressed by that.

We have to stop celebrating these people's money. We have to stop looking at them as leaders. We measure their success by how much money they made, and not how many children they let starve. I would like to see that calculation made every year when they publish the names on the Rich List.

The billionaires at least I can understand. The people who are not billionaires who defend them are the ones I don't get. 'Well, Wil, how much money is too much?' Um, let's start at having enough money to give everyone in history a dollar and work buck-wards. 'Well, Wil, they are not technically breaking any laws.' Okay, for starters you are always off to a good start when you have to throw *technically* in there. Is *technically* competing in the clean and jerk at the Olympics? Because it is doing some heavy lifting in that sentence. When someone runs the line that billionaires are not breaking any laws, I always feel like they are so close. 'They are not technically breaking any laws . . . because they are the ones that influence and set the laws . . . so the laws need to be changed for the benefit of everyone, not just them . . .' 'Oh, I see, it makes a lot of sense when you say it out loud.' It's not a compelling argument to say they are not doing anything against the law when they are the ones who came up with the law in the first place. 'The law of this house is that if you are going to have a sandwich then you have to give me half of your sandwich. It's the law!'

One of the main problems is that we equate money with intelligence. The person with the most money isn't necessarily the smartest; this isn't *Who Wants to Be a Millionaire?* If someone has a lot of money, we think they are more intelligent, which is stupid of us to think. Poor idiots. Sure, some smart people also have a lot of money, and we all know the climate scientists are loaded, but equating the two sends the message that if you are not doing well in life it is your fault, you deserve it, and that is how we justify not looking after the sick and poor and vulnerable. 'I did it, so why can't you? And I did it the whole way with this refreshing breeze at my back.'

I have heard people describe Jeff Bezos as a genius. Jeff Bezos is clearly a successful businessperson, but that doesn't make him a genius. I think the Apple Genius Bar has really devalued our expectations of what you need to be capable of to earn that title. Is Jeff Bezos a genius? Do you really think he is that much smarter than the people who work for him? Do you really think he works that much harder than the people who work in his warehouses? I am sure he has a lot on his plate, but I am pretty sure he still gets a bathroom break and doesn't have to piss in a bottle.

Just because someone is rich doesn't make them a genius, just as someone being poor doesn't make them an idiot. 'Hey, move over, Einstein. You may have worked out a theory of relativity. But you didn't work out that people like shopping. That's *real* genius. And I also discovered that they like their shopping delivered.' Let's give him the Nobel Prize. That is an idea that no-one in history had before him, and no-one probably ever would have had if he hadn't come along.

Genius.

Hey, here's a great idea for the world. Let's get the guy who looked at the most beautiful things in the world—bookshops—and thought, 'You know what, I think I know a way to ruin this,' and put him in charge of more things. I am sure everything will be *fine*. (And thank you, I guess, if you bought this book on Amazon. I get it: we might want to change the world but we also have to live in it. Jeff, sorry for the whole *Is he smarter than his workers? Does he work harder than them?* thing. I was just asking questions.)

We tell kids that they can't have their dessert until they have eaten their vegetables. We should hold billionaires to the same standards. You can indulge whatever rich-person fantasy you have with whatever money is left over when we are done fixing things. 'Yes, you can go to space and pretend to be an astronaut, but not until you have solved world hunger.'

The billionaires have traded in their super-yachts for super-rockets. They haven't, of course; they still have their super-yachts as well. They build them even bigger so they can spot them from space. How am I? I am not fine, thanks. I don't really understand why billionaires would want to travel to a different planet, seeing as they already live on a different planet from the rest of us. Some of them live in a different universe.

Sure, they might not *technically* be breaking any laws, but I can see that they are not paying enough tax. I don't need to see the books and the receipts when I can see the rockets. They are searching the universe not for signs of life, but for new tax havens. The plan is to find a new planet to settle and call it Panama 2.

If we really want to help the world, we don't need more billionaire space-tourists, but if they insist on going up, the least we can do is empty their bank accounts while they are up there. 'Yeah, we don't know what happened. While you were up there some apes took over and demanded we redistribute all your resources. They are not here now, they are all partying on your super-yacht with Jane Goodall. They also found the use of cartoon apes as currency to be offensive, so all the owners of those NFTs have been executed.'

I don't know if Jeff Bezos is a genius, but I do know what he is definitely not: an astronaut. Jeff Bezos is one of those people who had a layover at Heathrow airport and came home from holidays with a British accent. You know he is one of those people who is going to start every sentence for the rest of his life with, 'Well, when I was in *space* . . .'

When he returned from his first mission, which had all the gravitas of *Police Academy: Mission to Moscow*, Jeff said, 'The most profound piece of it, for me, was looking out at the Earth and looking at the Earth's atmosphere. Every astronaut, everybody who's been up into space, they say this, that it changes them.'

Well, it probably won't change you, Jeff, because you are not an astronaut. You're not even an 'independent astronaut'. You didn't go to space, you went to adult space camp. These billionaires are hanging out with actual astronauts who are operating the rockets and pretending they are the same thing. You are not. Flying first class on a plane doesn't mean you can land it in an emergency. 'Take my champagne, I am the captain now!'

He didn't go to space. Well, he did, *technically*. The *New Shepard 4* travelled 0.026 percent of the way to the moon. That is closer to the moon than I have ever been, but it doesn't make them Neil Armstrong. I could jump in the air and I am closer to the moon, but just like these 'astronauts' I am still, and this is a scientific term, a fucking long way away from the moon. I had a fake comedy club. They are fake astronauts. They dipped their toe in space, and I was higher than that in a photograph that was printed in the paper. I got higher than that on Doug Benson's show.

They were also only up there for ten minutes. That's barely enough time to listen to 'All Too Well' (Taylor's version) and from the footage of Bezos's first flight he spent most of it doing rolls and throwing around ping pong balls. You know, typical astronaut behaviour. I don't think Jeff Bezos is an astronaut; I think he is a *cat*. A tip to the employees of Amazon: if you want to negotiate a pay rise, I would suggest at the next negotiation with the boss you take in a ball of wool to distract him. Then take him out for sushi, he will love it.

He said, 'When you get up above [the atmosphere] what you see is, it's actually incredibly thin. It's this tiny little fragile thing. And as we move about the planet, we're damaging it.' Yes, Jeff, we are damaging it and by *we* I assume you mean you and the other billionaire robber barons who keep firing rockets into space. Jeff Bezos went to space for ten minutes and discovered that we are damaging the planet. Well, I guess all the fuss was worth it. I apologise. You are an astronaut, Jeff; you are Captain Obvious.

Jeff Bezos went to space and realised that we are damaging the planet. Well, that's climate change sorted then. As long as we can get every climate-change denier a rocket to space, we will be able to fix it after all. We pledge to get every denier and sceptic into space by 2050. (Actually we could solve some problems and some money by launching the deniers into space and not worrying about the return trip.)

By the way, I know it is possible to be changed by a moment. I have been changed by watching Sir David Attenborough talk about the Great Barrier Reef. Shit, sometimes I have had some pretty profound thoughts when I've had a little too much hip medicine and stared at the TV screen saver for too long. My problem is, the billions it cost for Jeff's trip would have bought enough food to stop tens of millions of people from starving, but I guess it was worth it for Jeff to have the revelation that the Earth is pretty. Yeah, he is a real genius.

We are so quick to judge conspiracy theorists for the dumb stuff they say. But we don't hold billionaires to account the same way. Yes, it's stupid that you think the vaccine is targeting professional soccer players, but that is not as stupid as a billionaire saying we are going to have colonies on Mars in a decade. At least Elon Musk dreams big, I guess. Jeff Bezos said, 'We can move all heavy industry and all polluting industry off Earth and operate in space.' Yes, he glimpsed the majesty of space, the galaxies and universe unfurling before him, and he thought, 'This place looks perfect for Bin Night.' Genius.

There's about as much of a chance the government is tracking us with microchips in the vaccine as there is that we will be living in space anytime soon. The main reason is simple: they can't make life more comfortable than it is on Earth (well, at least for those who can afford to make it into space). What's the selling point exactly? I wouldn't want to live in a tube where I can't wash on Earth, so why would doing it in space make it any more appealing? 'I have always identified as a space vampire, so a floating coffin is exactly what I am looking for, thank you. The other thing I love is suctioning my arse to things while I poo. Do you have anything that can help me with that?'

My favourite space fact is that apparently when you are up there you have to exercise two hours a day to stop your bones disintegrating and turning into sludge and goo. They are both technical terms; also Sludge and Goo are my second favourite New Zealand hip-hop outfit. Obviously your bones turning to mush (DJ Mush is on the wheels of steel for Sludge and Goo) is not too much of an issue on a ten-minute trip, but if you are living up there full-time you have to exercise two hours a day or Thunderbirds Are Goo. Thanks for the offer but I'm fine, thanks. I don't want to exercise that many hours a day on Earth.

If I can stop being cynical for a minute, and I am not sure I can, one good story that came out of the billionaire space race was Wally Funk. First, let's take a moment to give respect to one of the greatest names of all time. If you were going to a party and someone told you Wally Funk was going to be there, then you would know that was going to be a good party. Do you know what genre of music I never knew I loved until this moment? Wally Funk. Where's Wally? She's in space. (This joke probably doesn't work for international readers who know Wally as Waldo.)

If you don't know who Wally Funk is, and embarrassingly I didn't before she made headlines for being part of this trip, she was meant to be one of the first women in space. Back in 1961, she was part of a program and did all the training, but then the program got shut down for reasons I am sure had nothing to do with sexism. Some of the issues raised against the women's program were that: a) the moon would affect their cycle; b) the uniforms were white; and c) tampons were hard enough to use on Earth, so how would they insert them in zero gravity? The sad thing is, you don't know if that last sentence is true or not. It *sounds* like it might be true, right? Is it the truth or did I see it on the Tell Lies Vision?

The one upside to Jeff's vanity mission was that Wally Funk finally got to achieve her dream and go to space, well, space-*ish*. But it felt good for her, she deserved it, and I respected that Jeff Bezos had not only made her lifelong ambition a reality but made her, at 82, the oldest person ever in space—for one week, until Jeff took 90-year-old William Shatner up there and he broke Wally's record. That tells you everything you need to know about these flights: that the actual astronaut was surpassed by Captain Kirk. He boldly went where only an elderly lady had gone before.

Sir David Attenborough was almost 90 when he took a Triton to a depth of the ocean no-one had been before, and Wally Funk was 82 when she finally made it into space. I love that she made it. It is inspirational to never give up on your dreams, but I also love that 82 is the right age for someone to tell you exactly what they thought about the whole experience. And Wally had some thoughts. She was disappointed in the length of the flight (she hadn't even got the whole way through 'All Too Well'), and also the views. She said, 'We went right on up and I saw darkness.' I think she might have been describing Jeff with this comment.

'I thought I was going to see the world, but we weren't quite high enough.' I hear you, Wally. I have had that thought a few times in my life too.

I really can't wait for Wally Funk's Amazon review of the entire experience: 'Zero gravity was good for my arthritis but the cabin wasn't big enough for the rolls and twists, plus some idiot kept getting in my way because he was throwing Skittles into a billionaire kid's mouth . . . Two stars . . . which is about how many stars we could see from there.' She is Wally Don't Give A Funk.

By the way, I am aware I have spent a lot of time talking about billionaires in 'space' and I haven't mentioned the thing that most people immediately observed about Jeff Bezos's rocket, which was that it was extremely, how should we say, phallic in shape. Obviously I noticed—everyone noticed—but I didn't want to talk about it because I sincerely believe that's what they *wanted* us to talk about. It had to have been on purpose; no way was it accidental. There are just too many people who would have looked at the rocket before it launched for not one single person to notice. Not one person in the construction crew, not one person in mission control, not one astronaut, not one interested onlooker? I guess they could have noticed and been too scared to tell the boss, but I think it was on purpose. Yes, I know that most rockets are penis-like in shape, but this one may as well have had balls hanging off the bottom and veins up and down the sides. It wasn't a design flaw, it wasn't a mistake, it was on purpose. They wanted us to talk about the rocket looking like a dick to distract us from the pointlessness of it all. It was a distraction. It was a dick-straction. It was a dick inside a dick: a Turd-dick-can.

36

BANG

The longest I went between stand-up gigs was one year to the day. I know this because it was part of the reason I took the set in Brisbane: it would be exactly 365 days since I had last been on stage. There were a couple of catches. The first was that it was only a seven-minute spot, but it had an advantage over the previous seven-minute spot I had done as it had an *audience*. The bigger drawback was it was nearly three hours' drive to get there. It was going to be at least six hours' travel for seven minutes on stage. Luckily I had no other plans that day, week or month.

The drive up was uneventful, the gig went fine, not seven minutes in heaven but nice to be back playing my favourite instrument before a live audience, to once again get to surf the waves in that ocean, if only for seven minutes. But the drive home was a challenge. Not only was I tired, as the adrenaline wore off and the drive took its toll, but I was driving directly into a massive storm. Lightning was flashing, thunder was growling and the rain was streaming sideways. I was almost home when it happened, nearly six hours since I had left my house, driving carefully down the winding road.

BANG.

Sometimes life-changing moments do come with a bang.

Out of nowhere a giant branch, which had snapped off the tree above me, smashed my windscreen and bounced off the side of the road down the hill. The only thing that saved my life was that I didn't see it coming. If I had seen it for even a metre, my natural instinct would have been to swerve, and I would have gone off the side of the road and rolled down the hill and this story is over before it begins and there is no-one left to tell it anyway.

Luckily it was so sudden that I managed to not only drive calmly through it before I recognised what had happened, but even continued around a few corners before I could find a place to pull over and fully take it in. The minute I stepped out of the car and saw just how caved in my windscreen was, the proper panic started to set in as I realised how close I'd been to it all being over, for seven minutes of stand-up. I wouldn't even have died doing what I loved; I would have died *driving home* from doing what I love, and that doesn't sound anywhere near as romantic. Plus if there is one thing I am known for it is my desire to die peacefully in bed. This was so off-brand for me. I started to breathe heavily and just mutter to myself, 'Fuck. Fuck. Fuck . . . My immune system was right. The trees are trying to murder me. Why didn't I listen? I knew I shouldn't have moved the wood pile closer to the house.' I was not fine, thanks.

Before I knew it, I had left my car and started walking back up the road towards where the accident happened. I don't know what I was thinking. I guess I thought I was going to go back there and warn people or clear the branch away, but I was dressed in black, on a dark road, in the middle of the storm. I quickly realised that this is what horror movies would refer to as the Final Destination scenario, where I have already cheated death once and now I am walking back up the road. Yoohoo, Grim Reaper, over here!

I realised I needed to get home to safety as quickly as possible so I jumped back in the car and drove with my head poked out the window doggie-style. That's what that term means, right? I always assume when someone says they did it doggie-style they mean 'with their head poked out the car window'.

The minute I got home, I started ringing my friends. It was nearly midnight on a Saturday so the only friends who were awake were other comedians. 'You are not going to believe what just happened,' I said. 'I drove to Brisbane for a seven-minute gig, it took six hours and on the way home there was a massive storm and a branch fell on my car and I almost died!'

Every single one of my comedian friends asked the exact same first question: 'How was the gig?'

Yeah, I get it, it went fine, but not the point right now. This is the one time I do want you to ask me *how I am*.

The other thing I found curious was how many of my friends suggested I call the police. That seemed like a weird suggestion to me. I said, 'Yeah, what are they going to do? Arrest the tree? Call the special branch?'

I didn't want to call the police; I want to have a few stories that don't involve the cops. Plus what if I rang and they said, 'Hey, you're the guy who let those kids play *Grand Theft Auto*, aren't you? We've been looking for you.'

I didn't want to call the police, I wanted to call my doctor and say, 'Well, you were definitely right about how deadly that road is—much more dangerous than the vaccine.'

I didn't end up calling the police that night, but the next morning I decided I should do the right thing and at least report the details. I rang the Mullumbimby police station on Sunday morning and told my story, and I swear the policeman at the other end said, 'And so what would you like us to do, arrest the tree?'

I started laughing and said, 'That's what I told my friends. I mean, what are you going to do, call the special branch?'

There was silence at the other end of the line, so I thanked him and hung up.

The real reason I left the call to the cops until the next morning was that I had already had a run-in with police the night before. You see, on my way home from my seven-minute spot I had been pulled over . . . for a random drug test. I wasn't worried, I had not taken any medicine for more than 24 hours as I knew I had a long drive ahead of me and wanted to be at my most alert, but I am also not going to lie to you. As I pulled up to that RDT, I reached into my glovebox where I now keep a bottle of Apple Cider Vinegar. I swirled it in my mouth and passed the test. So I am not saying it *definitely* works, but I guess Do Your Own Research.

37

SPIKY

Probably my favourite moment of the last couple of years was seeing an echidna in my front garden. I had never seen an echidna in the wild before, let alone in my own garden. I had woken up with the sun, but had nothing planned for the day (and by day I mean week, and by week I mean month and, well, you get it). I decided to have some of my medicine and spend the day gardening. I don't know exactly how much medicine I had taken, but put it this way, my hips felt amazing and I certainly wasn't going to be operating any heavy machinery.

After a while I had built up quite an appetite from the gardening and the other green stuff. I went to the fridge for a snack and had a horrible realisation: I was out of snacks and now that I was medicated I couldn't get in the car to drive anywhere to get some. There was no amount of Apple

Cider Vinegar that could help my current situation. Living in the country, there is no food delivery service that comes to the house, and even if they did they would charge an extra danger fee for having to deliver down that winding road.

All that was in the fridge that even resembled a snack was some old dark chocolate wrapped in cling film. I couldn't even remember buying it, so I assumed someone else had been using it to cook and left the remainder in the fridge. It didn't technically belong to me, but it was in my refrigerator and there was no-one else there, so I figured I could probably eat it. It did not taste amazing, but I had the munchies enough that I still ate about half a block before I put the rest back.

I don't know when the echidna arrived or where it came from, because it was just there in the garden when I went back outside. It was literally sitting in a patch of cactus plants, which I thought was a pretty great hiding place for an echidna. To be honest, it may not have just arrived, it could have been sitting there for weeks and I just hadn't seen it move.

Not only was I seeing an echidna in the wild for the first time, but I had front row seats to the show. It was just there in my yard; that was as amazing to me as never seeing the musical *Hamilton* and then I walk out the front one day and Lin-Manuel Miranda and his mates are just belting it out amongst the cacti.

I watched it for a while, mesmerised by the way it moved its spikes. I realised that I really didn't know anything about echidnas. I mean, I knew they were native to Australia and they were on the five-cent coin, but other than that I really didn't know anything about them. I guess my brain thought that if they were really important they would have been on one of the more valuable coins. Maybe they should have had their picture on one side of the coin and some facts about them on the other side, although it would be tough to fit too many on the five cents, I guess.

I decided I needed to do some research. Yes, that's right, because of course there are some things that it is absolutely fine to do your own research about and googling 'echidna facts' fits that category. I don't think I am going to pick up too much echidna misinformation, and even if I did, what's the worst thing that would happen? 'I didn't take the vaccine because it is a plot by Big Echidna. Come on, you can't trust a mammal that lays eggs. They just want to inject you with their poison, that is why they are covered in needles! Come on, wake up, sheeple!'

So I started googling facts about echidnas. I knew that it would ruin my algorithm for a while. There was going to be a bot somewhere that thought, 'This guy seems to love echidnas. What can we sell him? Maybe an echidna we strap to his back that helps him with his posture.' But I was willing to take the risk because I needed to know more about this magnificent creature at my feet.

I knew some of the basics. I knew that it is a mammal that lays eggs, and it is a monotreme which I think means it only has one eyebrow. I didn't know echidnas are surprisingly good swimmers and use their snout as a snorkel. I discovered that when they hunt for food they make snuffling noises. Me too. Only half an hour ago I was snuffling through the cupboard and fridge looking for a snack until I found that disgusting cooking chocolate.

One thing I found interesting was that echidnas bury themselves when they are scared and threatened. In general, they don't have any natural predators because when they are threatened they just roll into a ball and hide. I get that. During the pandemic I definitely buried myself away from the world when I felt scared and threatened, and I am still in that hole. I am not sure I will ever come the whole way back. I have spikes to keep people at a distance—shit, I *am* an echidna. It also made me laugh that if echidnas bury themselves when they are scared, this little one clearly did not see me as a threat at all. Even an echidna had taken one look at me and decided it had me covered, and it was right. 'I have been here for 50 million years; I have seen dinosaurs, I have seen species come and go; I think I can handle you.'

As I continued to watch the echidna shuffle across the garden, I read more and more about them. One of the things I found most interesting was that apparently we don't know as much as we should about echidna mating because they refuse to mate in captivity. I respect that. I think I would have the same rule if I ever ended up in prison. Scientists have studied echidnas mating in the wild, but I like that they have drawn a line in the sand with their beak and said, 'If you want to watch us have sex, you perverts, you can come to us, we are not coming to you.'

It also means that in lab conditions, for us to be able to study their reproduction they need to be manually stimulated. When you hear someone is a scientist, you conjure this image in your head of them in a lab coming up with vaccines or developing solutions for climate change. You don't often think about the scientists in their lab having to manually masturbate an echidna. Which would be a tricky job because the echidna has a four-headed penis. (I will give you a moment now to go and google 'echidna penis'. Yeah, I know, right?) For those who didn't google, basically the penis is bright red and has four heads, and kind of looks like a dishwashing glove turned inside out. The penis isn't used for urination, so the theory is that they had the freedom to make it more elaborate. They say that two heads are better than one; well, the echidna has doubled that again. They only use two heads at once, but it's always good to have some spares on hand in case of emergency.

I also found out that a baby echidna is called a muggle, which couldn't be more adorable, and gives a whole new meaning to the Hogwarts franchise. Can't wait for *Harry Potter and the Four-Pronged Penis*.

The most amazing thing scientists have discovered about echidnas is that, instead of competing against each other, it seems that their sperm will work collaboratively. They will swim in bundles to get to the egg to give it the best chance of fertilisation. Apparently echidna sperm look at each other and say, 'We're all in this together.'

I'd been standing in my yard staring at an echidna and googling echidna facts for about 45 minutes when I said out loud to no-one, 'Why can't we all be more like echidna sperm?'

It was a weird thing to say out loud to yourself, although probably better than having other people hear it, when you think about it. I hope the poor echidna didn't know what I was talking about. 'See, this is why we won't breed in captivity. We don't want perverts like you talking about our sperm. Don't ask me about my sperm, and so you are clear, it is vaccinated. I am not scared of needles.'

As I thought about echidna sperm, my mind drifted to how much we rely on other people. Most days we have to trust people whether we think about it or not. Whenever you drive, you trust other people on the road to pay attention, not be intoxicated, not be looking at their phone or not just randomly swerve into your lane because they are having a bad day. When you go to a restaurant, you have to trust that the waiters have washed their hands and the chef hasn't just been fired and is sticking his dick in the sauces to celebrate. Every time you stand by the edge of a cliff or a bridge, you are trusting that the person standing behind you isn't going to push you over. You know that at least some of them are thinking about it. Even if they are good people who would never do it, you know it is going through their mind, and

I know it is going through their mind because that is what goes through my mind. There is the part of my brain that would never do anything like that, but there is the lower part of my brain that thinks, 'You know, you could just push them off right now!' And if you have never considered this before, I am sorry that it will now be on your mind every time you are on a bridge.

As I stared at my little spiky friend, a creature that has roamed the Earth for 20 to 50 million years, I couldn't help but compare it to human beings. Somehow I don't think we are going to make it to 20 million years. At this stage if you could *guarantee* me another 20 years I would probably lock it in. Humans think of ourselves as way above the echidna, but it was here before us and will probably outlast us too. We will continue to fuck things up and it will curl up in a ball and dig a hole. It saw us in, it will see us out. Of course, there are a whole bunch of species that won't see us out, but that is mostly *because* of us so I don't think we can take that as a victory.

Humans think we are so smart. We are so proud of ourselves, we've defeated our natural enemies and outsmarted our predators. But we didn't do that by being the strongest or the biggest or the fastest. We got there by working together, by forming communities and societies. That's what got us to the top of the food chain. If you know anyone who truly believes in the individual over society, take them to the zoo, and introduce them to each of the animals one on one in a fight. It's at least half the zoo. The animals are all so much faster, stronger and more venomous than we are. I wouldn't even need a big animal to do me in, I would get my arse kicked by anything more deadly than a medium-sized dog that hadn't had a walk that day. If zoos could only include animals that can be caught by one person, it would be 50 percent butterfly enclosure, two domestic cats and maybe a couple of lizards if the cats hadn't eaten them yet. We work when we work together. It's a lesson learned on the netball court: 'Here if you need!'

The echidna decided it was time to move on, but I wasn't quite done yet. So I started following it. Not in a creepy way. In a respectful way, from behind. Like I was walking behind a man carrying a tray of beers. If you love something, set it free. As I studied this magnificent prehistoric survivor, the way it moved was transfixing. 'You are awesome and you are doing great.' It made me think about how much time we spend trying to explore the cosmos when we sometimes don't appreciate the wonders that are here on the planet, from the Great Barrier Reef to my spiky four-headed-penis friend. He's spiky that is; the penis seems to have more of the texture of an old person who has been in the bath too long. Not that I touched the echidna penis, nor have I touched an old person who has been in the bath too long, so I may be way off on both counts.

I don't know if we are alone in the universe, but I know we have done some looking and we haven't found anything yet. We may be alone. An accident in the corner of the universe.

A literal once-in-a-lifetime offer. When I was at university I loved *The X-Files*. I even had the famous Mulder poster on the wall of my share house bedroom: 'I WANT TO BELIEVE'. But I don't think I do want to believe. I secretly suspect it's a good thing that if there are any aliens they haven't introduced themselves to us yet, because I really don't see how that would go well.

I am not so worried about them; I am worried about *us*. Do we really think we have our shit together enough as a civilisation to invite people over and show it off? I am not so sure. I think we need to fix some problems in this current relationship before we invite in a third. I don't think an external review would go too well. 'So you're in the middle of a global pandemic you are pretending is not happening anymore, you have life-saving medicine that people refuse to take because they trust a TV chef over a doctor, a handful of people own more than half the stuff while children starve, people are brainwashed daily by advertising messages, and climate change is a Code Red for humanity while your billionaires who could do something meaningful are jetting off into space. Oh, by the way, that is another thing: they didn't make it to space. We are from space and we didn't see them . . . Overall, humans are easily distracted but capable of so much if they would just apply themselves a little harder and not try to be funny all the time.'

As my echidna friend wandered away, all I could think was that we need to do better. Every person who has ever lived,

lived in a climate that no longer exists. We may be the only intelligent life in the universe and that means something. The Earth is 4.5 billion years old (but does not look a day over three billion to me), and we've been around for about 250,000 years (or 6000 years or whatever your definitely-not-a-conspiracy-theory says). The point is, we don't need to be in a rush to wrap things up. This is binge culture to the ultimate extreme. 'Come on, let's just skip to the end and see all the explosions!'

To put it simply, we don't need humanity to be the UK version of *The Office*. Yes, it was great but there are nowhere near enough episodes. We need it to be the US version of *The Office* and keep going and going. That echidna reminded me that the Earth is special. It's where all the people you love happen to live. Sure, all the people you hate live there too, but that is just part of the price we pay.

As I stood sobbing in my garden, I realised it was probably time to go inside. It had been a lot. I was overwhelmed and I didn't know exactly why. It wasn't one thing in particular. It was *everything*. Seeing that echidna had been a profound experience for me, and one I didn't need to fly into space to have. I didn't have to look up, I just needed to look down and pay attention. Plus, it had nearly been an hour I had spent in the garden with my new echidna mate and that was six Jeff Bezos space missions' worth of time. Yes, people can be changed by an experience. I stalked an echidna for 60 minutes and never looked at the world the same way again.

It was only months later that a friend who had looked after the house a couple of times said, 'Oh, I forgot to tell you, I left some magic mushroom chocolate in your fridge the last time I stayed here. Did you find that?' And I thought, well that explains a *lot*.

38

COW

We work because we work together. I was in Adelaide when the Northern Rivers of New South Wales flooded for the first time in 2022. When I had left home it was raining, but that was nothing unusual. It had been raining for months; it had barely stopped. 'Yes, Mr Serial Killer, I heard you the first time when you said you knew what I did last summer. I just need you to remind me what summer is again.'

It had been more than four months of pretty constant rain. My house is on a hill, which is helpful when it comes to flooding, but it also means the garden has a front lawn that is on higher ground near the road, and another lawn at the bottom of the hill. Usually when it rained, it would take one day of no rain for it to be dry enough to mow the top lawn, and two days of dry weather to mow the bottom. This time, after a while it was so wet it would take two days for the top lawn to dry and about four days for the bottom lawn, as more water ran down the hill into the uncut grass. This is how often it rained: in four months it was only ever dry enough for me to mow the top lawn and never once dry enough to mow down the bottom, so it just got wetter and wetter and longer and longer and more out of control. At the end of February when I left for Adelaide, if you had taken a photograph from above it would have looked like the house had a mullet. Business on the top lawn, party down below. It was wet, but there had been no warnings of what was to come.

I was at the Adelaide Fringe starting my first new tour since 2020, a show called *WILOGICAL*, when I found out what had happened. I woke up one morning and turned on ABC *News Breakfast*, but something was wrong with the television and instead it ended up on the *Sunrise* program. (I only ever watch the ABC, I didn't know there were any other channels and I am not just saying this because Ita has threatened to put down Bluey if I don't.) On *Sunrise* they were showing footage from Lismore where floodwaters were two storeys high and I saw an image of a cow on a roof. My first thought was, this is a fucked-up Cash Cow promotion and if I am about to see Sam Mac rescuing people in a tinnie then the breakfast television wars have finally gone too far.

You might not know this, but a cow on the roof is a bad sign. I don't expect you to be right across what cows do and don't do, but I can tell you this: I grew up on a dairy farm for the first seventeen years of my life and I didn't pay a lot of attention, but if there is one thing I did learn it is this: *Cows don't go on the roof.* They don't. If you see a cow on a roof something has gone majorly wrong in the world. But you never see it, because it doesn't happen. Cows don't go on the roof. It was so little of an issue on our farm that Dad never even brought it up, and his favourite topic of conversation was the things that can go wrong with the cows. It wasn't on his radar. Didn't crack a mention. Not once on a windy night did he ever say, 'You stay inside, children, it's blowing a gale and I have to go out there and tie down some cows.' We needed a trained dog to get them up a slight incline; we weren't worried about them climbing things. Okay, we did hear about one cheeky fucker that made it all the way over the moon, but I don't believe that and I haven't been able to find a peer-reviewed source to confirm it.

(Side note: There were some vaccinated people rescued from the floods too, so technically in the eyes of some in the community there were cows and sheep on the roof.)

One cow even made it to the beach. Sadly, this didn't end well, but I hope at least she enjoyed her day there. She probably would have been the first cow that ever made it to the beach. I hope she loved the feeling of the sand on her hooves, and in my mind I like to think she spent the day learning to surf and is still out there somewhere hanging eight and yelling, 'ME-a-bunga, dude!' Sometimes life-changing moments don't come with a bang, they come with a moo.

The cows weren't the only animals out of place. The floods were so bad there was a circle of sharks found in the streets of Mullumbimby. Luckily, it soon turned into a drum circle and no-one died because they all trusted their natural shark immunity.

But the truth is, we work because we work together, and suddenly a community that I had seen divided over two years came together. Their differences on other issues were put aside as they woke up each day and dedicated their lives to helping each other. Good people. It was amazing; they were *echidna sperm*. (Which is now officially the highest compliment I can give any group of people working together.) One of my favourite stories of the floods was the news that surfing champions Joel Parkinson and Mick Fanning were out on their jet-skis rescuing people. The next day Mick Fanning backed up and became an unpaid Uber service to transport emergency workers and vets to work. Five stars, Mick Fanning. Imagine getting a ride to work through a flood with Mick Fanning! He could be the coolest bloke in the world. He didn't look at the floods and think, 'That's not my job.' He *did* something. 'Yeah, it's been a busy day actually, went for a surf with a cow this morning and now I am doing this for the rest of the day.' You would feel in safe hands: if you ran into a shark he could just punch it out of the way.

The community were amazing. Emergency services weren't responding fast enough, so people were literally crowdfunding helicopters. I would have thought this was the perfect time for the government to take some of those helicopters they regularly fly over that part of the world anyway to check if anyone is growing some *medicine* in their backyard, and finally put them to good use. They already know the area. 'Captain, we need to turn left at the house where the guy has three plants he has tied some tomatoes to and thinks he is fooling us, and then take a left at the house that looks like it has a mullet.'

I knew I needed to get home, but I couldn't, as everything was cut off: the airports, the roads, the internet and phone lines. The floods had destroyed the entire 5G network, which I guess would have been one good piece of news for some locals in a tough time. People were stranded and they couldn't call for help. Even in the places where people could access supplies, they could only pay for fuel and food with cash and there was no cash left in the ATMs and no internet to transfer money. Everything was cash, which to be fair wasn't much of a change of policy for many of the local businesses. But it meant that when I did get home, I needed to bring cash with me and there is absolutely nothing suss about withdrawing hundreds of dollars of cash in the middle of the night on the final night of a festival. No red flags in my bank account at all.

39

FLOODS

We work when we work together. When we look out for each other. It's netball, here if you need. Of course, the community had no other choice but to work together, because everyone else was doing what I believe is known in scientific circles as Fuck All. (Or Fa on the periodic table. Again, calm down, nerds, I know that is Faradium.) During the pandemic there were many times, from masks to vaccines, when I thought, 'Why don't these people trust the government?' And then something goes wrong, and the government does fuck all. Well, I guess maybe they had a point.

The locals asked why there had been no warnings that these catastrophic floods were coming and the authorities said, 'We didn't have a crystal ball.' You know what? I would accept that answer anywhere but the Northern Rivers of New South Wales. There are crystal balls everywhere up there.

They come standard in every room. In case of emergency, break glass and consult crystal ball. It's harder to find a ball that *isn't* made of crystal. I have one on my key-chain. I am pretty sure there was a guy juggling crystal balls in the room where the authorities made that statement, and I definitely spotted at least one spirit level.

The community needed to look out for each other because the army took time to arrive and then, when they did, their camouflage was working so well it looked like they weren't there. I don't blame the people on the front line, by the way, it's not their fault. They can't flick on *Sunrise*, see a cow on a roof, grab a tank and roll out. But I do blame the people in charge who claimed that the ADF is not available at a moment's notice. That is a great message to send about our armed forces. 'Hey, enemies, I know we are a land of enormous wealth with a land mass so huge and a population so small that we could never defend it . . . so if you are going to try and invade, could you please have the courtesy to give us a heads-up so we can get our shit together? About 50 years is probably enough notice—we might even have some submarines by then, which will be good when everything is under water.'

To be fair, the defence minister at the time started a GoFundMe page and as defence minister of the country, what more could he do? I guess we should be grateful he didn't see the images of people getting rescued in tinnies and try to stop the boats. Where are the people of Lismore now? They got sent to Christmas Island. That's always been a bad policy, but even more so now because we could really do with those boats. Our new policy should be that you can come to Australia in a boat as long as you bring an extra boat. We even have a new job for you: taxi driver in Lismore.

The community needed to come together because the government did fuck all. They refused to access money from their disaster emergency fund, saying they were saving it for a rainy day, which seemed to be a weird way to phrase it in the middle of a once-in-a-lifetime flood. The saddest thing about that was realising they know that there are going to be days that are rainier than this, and they are not doing enough to stop them. They know we are going to look back on this as the good times. 'Hey, everyone, remember back in 2022 when there was only one cow on our roof?'

The most frustrating truth is that if we don't do some-thing, these *are* the good times. The weather is like the *Fast & Furious* sequels: it is just going to get more and more extreme. The message we get from our leaders is that we need to adapt to more regular disasters. 'Come on, people, we can't make any of you happy, can we? A couple of years ago you were complaining that everything was on fire, and now you are complaining that everything is flooded. All that water certainly put out any fires. Can't you be grateful for that? Look at the glass as half full. If you want to continue to live in a flood zone, then the best advice we can give you is to adapt and start growing gills. You can't expect the government to keep handing out cash if you are not willing to grow a couple of gills. If we don't see the gills you don't get the bills.'

Yes, we need to adapt, of course we do, but what are the animals going to do? Do they have to adapt too? What about birds that are being knocked out of the sky by hailstones the size of cricket balls? Do they need to adapt a sidestep? Do they need to talk to the goose about it? What about koalas, what are they meant to do? They are losing their habitat. Do they need to adapt too? Next time they meet a visiting celebrity, should they ask to be taken home to their mansion? Or should they pick their pockets? Those claws do look perfect for grabbing a wallet out of a suit pocket. And what about cows? Do they need to adapt to living on the roof? You think possums are noisy—wait until you've got a couple of Friesians up there.

Of course, this message shouldn't be surprising from the same government that had blamed the bushfires not on climate change but on arsonists. At least it is much harder to run that line when it comes to floods: 'Yeah, we don't know what happened. We just woke up and Lismore was completely under water. We think some teenagers snuck in with some long hoses and filled up the town.' You know that excuse is not true, because there are no long hoses in the Northern Rivers. Of course, the fires and the floods *were* caused by arsonists: they just wear suits and work for the fossil fuel companies.

We work because we work together, but even in times like these there are those who would blame the victims. I heard people say, 'Well, people shouldn't live in flood zones if they don't want it to flood.'

Hey, dickhead, you know why people live in flood zones? They live there because it is affordable housing. And you know why it is affordable? Because it's in a flood zone. When the real estate agent said 'water views', they didn't mention that those views would be of water in the living room and the kitchen. But I will say, this is a nice kitchen.

40

BRIDGE

The night of the second Northern Rivers flood, I know exactly where I was. I was on stage at a fundraiser to raise money for victims of the first flood. It was almost a month to the day from the original flood and it turns out Mother Nature heckles hard. My first thought, as it started to rain so heavily it didn't sound like rain anymore and became white noise, was: 'Well, I guess the government was right, there were rainy days ahead.'

(Side note: The Wiggles ended up performing at a fundraising gig for the flood victims as well, and if we can't get Australians to care about the natural disasters themselves, can we at least convince them that if we keep having them we are going to kill off The Wiggles?)

I will say it's an unusual feeling to have a once-in-a-lifetime weather event happen to you twice in a month. I guess the main feeling is blessed, right? I mean, when I was young, people only got to experience once-in-a-lifetime weather events, you know, once in a lifetime. But up my way, they are like John Farnham farewell concerts: if you miss this one there will be another coming along soon. 'Oh no, when we said once in a lifetime we didn't mean a *human* lifetime. We were talking more the lifetime of a house fly—about a month.'

As it poured, my thoughts were of the flight I was meant to be taking to the Melbourne International Comedy Festival the next day. The 2020 festival would have been my 25th year in a row and now I was returning with my brand-new show *WILOGICAL* for the first time since then. Or was I? First I needed to make it home from the fundraiser and that was going to present some problems. Before the first flood there were two roads from my house, turn left or right at the front gate, they were the options. After the original flood hit, there was only one way out, as the road to the left had been completely destroyed by landslides in some places and in others the cracks in the road were so big it looked like there had been an earthquake instead of a flood. How big were the cracks? Well, put it this way: if the road were a cricket pitch, you would definitely play three spinners and not want to bat on the final day.

The water had also washed the sides of the roads away and the more they were used the more they crumbled and frayed at the edges. It got to the point where the side of the road was so dangerous, when you passed a car coming in the other direction, for you both to stay on the road you would have to drive so close to each other you could high-five. I didn't, of course; that is dangerous. I didn't even wind my window down. I thought that with my luck that is how I would get Covid. I would pass someone and they would cough and I would be the first person to get Covid in a drive-by.

The problem with the road turning left being destroyed was that that was where the local store and coffee shop live, where the mail is delivered. They think it will take years to repair the damage and open it again. I feel most sorry for the little coffee shop, because during the pandemic I think I had been keeping them in business. I fear that they won't be able to survive without me. It wouldn't surprise me if one morning we wake up and the road has been completely rebuilt. People will ask, 'Who did that, the council?' No, it was *baristas*.

The road to the left was completely destroyed, but there was also a problem with the road to the right, the winding back road into Mullumbimby. It mainly had to do with a bridge that was there before the flood and nowhere to be seen afterwards. I like to think it was somewhere on a beach hanging out with a surfing cow. It was only a small bridge, but without it we were completely cut off from the outside world. After a day or two it was clear that in the grand scheme of emergencies in the area, it was probably a low priority and no-one was going to be able to come and fix it. So then the locals did something amazing: they got together and they built a bridge.

I don't know how they learned how to build a bridge; I imagine they must have done their own research. But build a bridge they did, out of rocks and gravel and cement and pretty much anything that they could find. There was a gang of volunteers young and old and they built a bridge. In some ways it was a very Northern Rivers bridge. It was a handmade, rock-to-hole, artisanal bridge experience. I know what you're thinking. Can a group of locals make a homemade bridge that works like an actual bridge? Well, you'll be pleased to know the answer is . . . *almost*. Close. It was very bridge-like, bridge-adjacent. Put it this way: if your preschool kid drew a picture of this bridge you would think they were a genius, and you would put it straight on the fridge. 'This is a fridge-bridge,' you would say to your preschool Picasso. But if your architect brought you the same drawing of a bridge, you would at the very least ask for a second draft thanks, Tiger.

To be perfectly clear, I am not mocking the bridge or the people who made it. I found it so impressive that they literally MacGyvered up a bridge out of nothing and connected people to their lives, loved ones, jobs and supplies. They were heroes in my eyes and it was certainly better than any bridge that would have been built if I had been left in charge. My plan would have been: 'Well, the bridge is gone, so I guess we just have to stay here until there is a drought and then we will drive over the river bed hoping the fires don't catch us in the meantime.'

It may not have looked like a perfect bridge, but it did the job a bridge was meant to do. At least for a while. It was really good at being a bridge right at the start, and then the more people drove over it, the less it looked like a bridge; and then it started to rain again as I drove over that bridge on the way to my fundraiser gig and I wondered if it would be there when I got back. It was, but I think I may have been the last person to ever drive across it, because when I went to leave to go to Melbourne early the next morning, the bridge was gone.

The Melbourne International Comedy Festival in 2020 and 2021 was ruined by Covid. I didn't expect 2022 would be ruined by the other Big C, climate change. (I guess technically the Big CC, which could also be Cancel Culture or corn chips and now I have forgotten the point I was trying to make and regret medicating before writing this bit.) I ended up missing the first week of the festival because I was trapped in my second once-in-a-lifetime flood. But compared to most I knew, I was lucky. I remember dropping off some food to a shelter in Lismore when we finally got out and I was having a chat to a guy who worked there about how he was going. I asked if he had lost much in the second flood and he replied, 'No.' That seemed like some good news so I said, 'That's good news,' and he replied, 'I didn't lose anything in the second flood because I lost everything in the first one.' That's why I don't ask someone how they are unless I am prepared to hear the answer.

I eventually made it back to the Melbourne International Comedy Festival. I made a few jokes about the community I lived in, but I wouldn't have been able to make any of those jokes without that same community. Because when the water went down, there may have been no bridge, but what was left was resilience and each other. That community, like the band Chumbawamba, got knocked down, but they got back up again. and they built another bridge and this time the bridge was even better than the first. They had learned from that, they had adapted. This time they built a ridgy-didge-fridge-bridge and it was glorious to behold, not just the bridge itself but the way it was put together. Everyone was down there helping, and when I say everyone I mean everyone. We work when we work together.

There were older people, kids and one person in particular loading a rock into a hole who caught my eye: it was my wood thief. That made me feel better about letting him go. See, everyone deserves a second chance. I knew he was a good person at heart. I felt pretty smug driving away until the thought occurred to me that he was probably down there stealing rocks. 'Hey, Wil, actually while you are here, can you help me load these into the back of my ute?'

ACKNOWLEDGEMENTS

I'd like to thank Kelly and Malcolm and the team at Allen & Unwin for their patience and advice, and Kevin, Dioni, Kath and the team at Token for being there for my bullshit.

QUOTED WORKS

With grateful acknowledgement to those who wrote the artistic works quoted in this book:

p. 23—'Faith', *Faith*, 1987, performed by George Michael, written by George Michael, Sony Music Entertainment.

p. 23—'Wake Me Up Before You Go Go', *Make It Big*, 1984, performed by Wham!, written by George Michael, Columbia.

p. 29—'It Takes Diff'rent Strokes', 1978, written and performed by Al Burton, Gloria Loring and Alan Thicke, NBC.

p. 56—'Forgot About Dre', *1999*, 2001, performed by Dr. Dre and Eminem, written by Andre R. Young, Marshall Mathers and Melvin Bradford, Aftermath.

p. 69—'In the Navy', *Go West*, 1979, Village People, performed by Village People, written by Henri Belolo, Jacques Morali and Victor Willis, Scorpio Music.

p. 72—'My Country', 1908, Dorothea Mackellar, Dorothea Mackellar Estate.

p. 171—'Santa Claus Is Comin' to Town', 1934, written by J. Fred Coots and Haven Gillespie, Leo Feist Inc.

p. 184—*The Princess Bride*, 1973, William Goldman, Bloomsbury, London.

p. 215—'Hot In Herre', *Nellyville*, 2002, performed by Nelly, written by Chuck Brown and Cornell Haynes, Jr., Motown/Sony Music Publishing/Warner Chappell Music.

p. 226—'We Built This City', *Knee Deep in the Hoopla*, 1985, performed by Starship, written by Bernie Taupin, Dennis Lambert, Martin Page and Peter Wolf, Rhino/Universal Music Publishing.

p. 227—'Read About It', *10, 9, 8, 7, 6, 5, 4, 3, 2, 1*, 1982, performed by Midnight Oil, written by Robert Hirst, James Moginie, Peter Garrett, Martin Rotsey and Peter Gifford, Columbia.